COMPETING IN THE CONNECTING WORLD

COMPETING
IN THE
CONNECTING
WORLD

THE FUTURE OF YOUR *DISRUPTED* INDUSTRY
IS ALREADY HERE

GREGG GARRETT & WARREN RITCHIE

LIONCREST
PUBLISHING

WRITTEN BY GREGGORY R. GARRETT & WARREN T. RITCHIE

COMPETING IN THE CONNECTING WORLD

The Future of Your Industry Is Already Here

ISBN   978-1-5445-1109-2 *Paperback*

         978-1-5445-1110-8 *Ebook*

CONTENTS

FOREWORD AND ACKNOWLEDGMENTS

We have written this book for tomorrow's leader—for those who are not content simply being part of an organization but would rather shape its future. We do not claim that all the ideas are original, nor that all the models are complete, but they have proven valuable to the two of us and countless clients, colleagues, and friends. What you are about to read are observations, patterns, and proven techniques that we have shaped over fifteen years of working and advising together and the decades individually prior. We are hoping to assist you in beginning your journey in transformation. A journey that will require perspective and bravery. A journey of leadership. A journey to compete in the connecting world.

Although we have documented the material, we could not have done it without the support of many. We would like to recognize many of you who have helped in our journey. We are certain we will inadvertently omit some who have helped shape our professional perspectives. No matter if you supported in our careers, our learnings, or in our lives, we thank you.

Specifically, Warren would like to acknowledge:

Many of the core ideas in this book are borrowed from the work of others. Gregg and I have chosen not to cite the sources of the ideas simply to make the book easier to write and potentially to read. However, in these brief following paragraphs, credit is given to but a few of the others who have been influential about some of the thoughts behind the book. A full list would require much more effort.

The premise of the book—that a technological discontinuity will disrupt the status quo of industry—is an application of the punctuated equilibria model developed by Niles Eldridge and Stephen Jay Gould. Richard Bettis assigned his strategy doctoral students, including myself, readings in the areas of physics and biology in order to discover that natural science models fit well in explaining the socially constructed world of industry. Howard Aldrich's seminar on the social forces underlying the origins, functioning, and disbanding of organizations has also been highly influential. Two decades ago, I worked for Clive Warrilow, a CEO at the time, who imparted on me the idea that the "car business" was really quite simple, and the industry was ripe for disruption, the problem being that the people necessary to enact a transformation are burdened with the personal belief that the business was actually highly complex and that their identities were wrapped up in that complexity. Years later, I found that phenomenon actually had a published name—the industry dominant logic—and that the above-mentioned Richard Bettis is co-credited with naming it. I also recall Gerd Klauss, another CEO, who was proficient at turning a clever phrase, use the term, "fortune favors the prepared" (from Louis Pasteur). I always have found that phrase to be a useful answer to the question, "Why bother to spend time to think about transforming organizations?"

Thinking about and working at organizational change has engrossed me at times during my life to the exclusion of thought of other important matters. The time spent pursuing a career has frequently kept me apart from the most important people in my life. So now, inside the opening pages of this book are a few words to express the pride and love I have for family: Warren King and Shirley, Laura and Adam, Dawn, Les and Leah, and to my love and best friend, Viara, whom I admire for all she has achieved in her own right and who has been so loving, patient, and supportive of me.

Last, this book would never have made it to publication without the enthusiasm and persistence of my coauthor, Gregg. Writing this book was his idea. He convinced me that the concepts, experiences, and metaphors that we have developed and exchanged for years are worth offering to a wider audience in the context of the connecting world. Further, that by publishing them, maybe someone somewhere will do something different and maybe that will make some difference.

Specifically, Gregg would like to acknowledge:

Many of my professional colleagues and clients have helped to shape my perspective on this book's subject matter. I am grateful to each of them. Specific thanks are given to Ed Rybicki for changing the course of my career by recruiting me to Volkswagen and introducing me to Dr. Warren Ritchie; Eric Verniaut for trusting a very young "kid" to take on responsibilities beyond my years and setting up my deep dive into exploring the strategic nature of the Connected World; John Horn and his entire T-Mobile USA M2M team for including me as one of their own, exposing me to so much of the business of IoT, and for teaching me the value of being the "easiest with which to do business"; Oliver Riedel for supporting innovative bravery and protecting it from cultural antibodies long enough for me to feel the disruptive potential of connected technologies; my past colleagues who have trusted my gut, proven where I was right and where I was wrong, and put up with my long-winded discovery sessions that eventually led to this book; the entire CGS Advisors team and alumni for the continued encouragement and interest in the subject. It is all the CGSers who bring the "First Mile" to life for clients, and without you, this story would not have been written.

Additional appreciation goes to Dr. Bob Vantil and the Oakland University Schools of Business and Engineering for encouraging me to develop and teach the graduate-level "Competing in the Connected World" course; to the hundreds of students who have attended classes and lectures and helped us refine the observations and models presented in this book; to my professional friends who have guest lectured, discussed the content, and challenged our ideas for many years: Tim McCabe, Ty Beltramo, Chris Pesola, Jeff Poiner, Stephan Tarnutzer, and Emmett Romine. Huge kudos go to Dr. Mohan Tanniru and Dr. Graeme Harper for lending their perspective to the publishing process and experience as authors. Tara Taylor, thank you for assisting us in getting the writing process started, and to the Lion Crest Publishing team for helping us get it finished. Deep gratitude for Avner Landes and Jeremy Brown for guiding this path.

To my friend, colleague, mentor, and coauthor, Dr. Warren Ritchie, thank you for sharing in the intellectual curiosity and commitment to the process that has developed this book.

The most special appreciation goes to my family. Russ, Dorothy, and JoAnn, I appreciate that you helped to set a foundation. D'Anne, you always encouraged me, were my number one supporter, and prepared me for the future. Thank you for all you have done. Spencer and Caleb, your inquiries about the process, the topic, and "When will it be done?" cheered me on to be an "author." Thank you for sharing "our time" so I could write. This book is for you. Of course, a deep sense of gratitude is reserved for my wife, Amy. Thank you for pushing me to explore new adventures and for constantly managing life while I have worked, written, and grown. Thanks for being my partner as we prepare to live in this Connected World. I love you!

Last, to you, the reader, thanks for trusting us to give a perspective on your journey. I hope that we can help you reflect, be brave, and truly be prepared to compete in the connecting world.

INTRODUCTION

THE FUTURE IS ALREADY HERE

In the decade ahead, Manuel, recently promoted to the position of CEO, will be sitting in his redecorated corner office attempting to prepare for an onslaught of afternoon meetings. Instead of processing through his backlog of reports, he may find himself admiring the fork in his hand. It may look identical to the fork we use today, but in this near future this fork has features and abilities far greater than merely being able to hold the weight of the food on its tines. This connected fork has come a long way since its "haptic fork" predecessor was first introduced to the public in the early 2010s. Then it was just a chunky gadget whose value was limited to measuring the rate at which the user ate, relaying the data to an app through Bluetooth. Occasionally, it would vibrate to remind the user to slow down in order to give his stomach time to signal to his brain that he was full.

In the intervening decades, sophisticated sensors were embedded into the utensil. The version Manuel may someday hold in his hand will likely measure the nutritional and caloric content of the food he's putting into his body. Without having to lift a finger, the fork will send the data to his health-care provider, dietary planner, grocery delivery service, and physical trainer, parties that have a particular interest in this information. His insurance company may even reduce his premium if he can keep consuming nutritional content that is customized to his specific body makeup through DNA analysis.

The use of sensors in thousands of everyday products, such as the haptic fork, office chairs, wearables, and refrigerators, will change health care. It will no longer be a backward-looking industry dealing with crises after they happen. The connected toilet will likely have the ability to analyze urine and provide an up-to-the-minute report on your body's chemistry. A complex ecosystem of connected devices and accompanying services will constantly monitor your daily activities, allowing you, with the assistance of your health-care professionals, to take a proactive approach to your medical care.

Instead of a once-a-year physical, you may find value in

having your health care woven into your daily life. For instance, as Manuel completes his lunch and walks to his 1:00 p.m. meeting, he gets notified that his sugar intake is over the appropriate level (that damn bagel from the accounting department's "bagel club," which he was encouraged by his head of Human Resources to join). A pop-up message on his mobile "phone" suggests that a short period of exercise will return him to the healthy zone. Seeing that his schedule is flexible later in the day, Manuel's health service automatically alters his preferred autonomous transportation pickup location, moving it two miles away from the office, which will provide him with both time and opportunity to exercise while allowing him to still make his son's soccer match on time. A simple thumb swipe approves the changes.

Later that afternoon, with his meetings finished, Manuel strolls the two miles and reflects on the seamlessness of this experience and the overall state of technology. Suddenly, an overwhelming surge of fear grips Manuel. Every device in his office and on his person, from complex machines, such as his personal bot assistant and cloud-based computer, to simple items, such as the fork and the 4-D printed shoes he is wearing, is connected. They're collecting information, not only to enhance the experience of using the devices but also to benefit other services and products in his life. They're not only internet-connected and "smart" but also starting to connect with one another in order to make their services more relevant.

What does this connected landscape mean for the future of Manuel's business, especially because his predecessor and the entire previous generation of leadership never took steps to modify the product or services and prepare the company and the way it operates for this Connected World?

He likely shares some of the blame, too. The signs of the Connected World were clear when he started out on the executive track a decade ago. He saw how complex devices such as jet engines, manufacturing equipment, and cars were embedded with sensors to collect data on their usage and performance. Soon, he witnessed the emergence of smart thermostats, televisions, and thousands of other everyday products that recorded data, but they were all just one-off experiences that rarely resulted in tremendous value.

He failed to see the speed at which this technology was disrupting industries. Start-ups such as Uber and Airbnb managed to disrupt entire industries in the span of several years. As a senior leader moving through the ranks of his organization, he was always trying to prove to the other executives that he fit in. He helped ensure that their product stayed a market leader for that era, while never preparing it for the future. Yes, they made a connected version of their product, and even offered a "premium" version that included a monitoring service of the product, but they never truly transformed their company. After all, his company produced a less-complex product, meaning he didn't feel an obligation to address this potential disruption in a profound way. Instead of seeing these connected products and services as the future, he chose to see them as novelty items, cute ways for companies to sell more of their standard products. So his company, along with everyone else, installed a sensor and connected some products with a focus on making simple features available remotely and reducing costs of the traditional industrial world. Consideration of how this data may reshape the customer's experience or the overall company was not fully understood or deeply considered. Manuel and the other leaders at the company never attempted to monetize the data or tried forming partnerships with companies that could find value in the information.

THE TIME TO PREPARE IS NOW

The above scenario isn't science fiction. It's the future, and you and other business leaders across all industries are already seeing the seeds of this connecting world. Preparing for the change now, or like Manuel, waiting until the industries have already shifted, is your choice.

It's likely that in a matter of years, you'll witness the emergence of this new landscape, one where formerly discrete things will be a part of integrated ecosystems. The haptic fork that will provide real-time data to doctors and health insurers is only one example. What this means is that discrete products with limited connectivity will be insufficient to maintain a growing business. Almost every thing will become part of the internet of everything, and the value of products and services will be determined by the seamlessness and usefulness of their connections to other products and services in the user's life.

Maybe you consider these issues real but feel that these somewhat futuristic challenges are better left to your successor. After all, you aren't currently feeling the effects of a potential disruption on your bottom line. Looking out at the current competition and trends in the industry, it may be hard for you to find a reason to start tampering with a business model that, by all indications, has the company performing optimally and is satisfying the board and investment communities.

Nevertheless, if you want to get a sense of how fast a business's health can change once technological discontinuities begin to take shape, look at how industries are being impacted when companies choose to focus on "share economy" business models. Talk to taxi drivers, car dealerships, and car manufacturers about the impact of ride sharing companies (e.g., Uber, Lyft, etc.) on their industries.

Companies such as Uber and Lyft have built a business model focused on moving people (and goods) from point A to point B. Relying on outside devices to connect the consumer to the vehicle and its driver, it has created a platform business that is slowly altering car ownership. In the next decade, autonomous cars will further enhance these business models by disintermediating the human from operating the vehicle, reshaping the way cars are bought, sold, and used. Private ownership of vehicles will dramatically decline. Instead, a transportation company may own a massive fleet of vehicles. This development alone will leave the major players in the capital-intense car manufacturing industry scrambling to react to disintermediation from their end customer. The mechatronics of the vehicle will change now that each vehicle will have to cater to the needs of potentially thousands of different riders, who may be using the vehicle for periods no longer than twenty minutes at a time. All this disruption could stem from a set of companies that are less than a decade old.

THE INTERNET OF THINGS WILL BEGIN TO CHANGE EVERY THING

The Internet of Things (IoT) is a collective set of technologies that, when assembled together, act as a key building block on our path to the Connected World. IoT is the networked connection of embedded computing technology placed in objects that enable them to send and receive data autonomously. IoT is a set of building blocks that, when applied together, reshape the way information can flow. If managed properly, this flow of information can drive new value for the product user, the product owner, and the product manufacturer. In fact, this new product-in-use (PiU) data will build bridges to adjacent product and service experiences, helping to drive new ecosystems and paths to value. We will explore these complex changes in greater detail throughout the book. As things are produced and connected to send and receive information, they will act as a disruptive force to your industry. The only question is when you and your firm will first feel the disruption and whether it will be too late to react.

IoT is the linkage of two vastly different worlds: the Internet world and the Thing, or product, world. Leaders of product companies who were raised in the "things" industries will often view IoT as an extension of their product strategy and a way to enhance their product experiences. Most often, these leaders work with their company's engineers or IT staff to connect the thing (T) that they make to the network, usually through embedded computing or sensors. This new embedded technology can record, disseminate, and receive data, and command the device to behave differently. Leaders who have learned patterns from digital or Internet (I) firms will often see the connected product simply as a platform for a digital service or experience, often underestimating the complexity of the design, production, or distribution of the product itself.

Ultimately, these connected products must add value to the user, owner, or producer of the thing. Sometimes, the value will only be recognized if the product is connected to other things and services. How much value is there, for example, in a user knowing whether he or she is eating too fast versus the fork connecting to the rest of a person's nutritional, activity, and health ecosystems? It will be more about ensuring a seamless experience between products and services.

What leaders will soon discover is that this fairly simple added technology will cause your company, which was at one time squarely in an established industry, to compete in a blended, connected industry. The company will need to merge "Things" norms, such as structure and way of thinking, with the "Internet" norms from digital firms. This likely will be a paradigm shift for most companies that are coming from a world of disconnected experiences and discrete products and entering one where all products, services, and the accompanying experiences are linked. Welcome to the era of the next technologically driven discontinuity.

The shift from product-only businesses to products *and*

services businesses, or even just services businesses, will have a major impact on the entire structure of your company and the industry it's a part of. Consider the effort it may have taken a product company to enter its industry pre-IoT. The company may have had to invest in manufacturing, retail centers, warehouses, and logistics infrastructure. In the IoT era, one company's product can become another company's platform. Compare a privately owned Mini Cooper to a Zipcar by Hertz-enabled Mini Cooper. The difference is an inexpensive electronics module added to the vehicle that allows for Zipcar subscribers to interact with the vehicle so they can unlock the doors using their mobile phones. Zipcar didn't need to design, engineer, manufacture, or distribute the car. They used software and a subscription model to disintermediate customers from the car company. These low costs of entry allow companies possessing emerging technologies and business models to move much faster than traditional businesses. In this new environment, it's not an exaggeration to say that any college dropout working in his or her garage can take on industry titans. With one small increase in value to an established product, through the data it produces, start-ups or industry laggards can swiftly pull customers away from industry leaders, meaning your company can be the one displacing others, or it can be the one that's ultimately displaced.

A common mistake is thinking you can take your time

adapting to this new reality because you have current market share on your side. Customers are constantly on the move. In the IoT-enabled era, customers are loyal to the extent that they don't have a better alternative. Take the case of Myspace, which from 2005 to 2009 dominated the social networking world. More than a hundred million users invested time in creating profile pages and establishing personal networks. Nevertheless, in the span of a couple of years, tens of millions of these users migrated to an upstart called Facebook.

AN INTERNET OF THINGS LEADS TO A CONNECTED WORLD

The IoT is reaching buzzword status. Its usage has become as common as "cloud," "AI," "autonomous," and the holy grail, "digital." It comes in the form of a new name such as "Smart" followed by a term such as "manufacturing" (smart manufacturing). Some industry leaders understand the massive disruptive potential and are focusing on an X.0-type framing of their industry. An example of this would be "Industry 4.0," which has become the term, born in Germany and extending to Asia and now the United States, for the digitization of the traditional manufacturing supply chain. Other industries are simply referring to their product name with the term "connected" added as a prefix (e.g., Connected Car). Regardless of what it is called, the technology advancements are driving significant change and requiring firms to rethink their strategies, or their "Digital Strategies."

Yes, IoT is, at its core, an incredible collection of technologies. The focus and decisions for leaders, however, must be much broader than simply technological. They must understand that the systems in question are more complex than that of one product and the connection enabling it. They must understand that the Connected World is a set of ecosystems made up of many products and many connections. They must also comprehend, when preparing their business for IoT and its disruptive potential, that the true recipient of value remains The People.

The first thing that fifty percent of the population of North America does in the morning, before they pick up a cup of coffee, kiss their spouse, check on their children, use the restroom, or take a shower, is check a mobile device. People seek information. People push out information. People react to information from humans and machines. Our society is already connected, and it's only getting more connected as more and more information is being produced, captured, and transferred.

People have been connecting for many years. Thousands of years ago, a person's "world" likely revolved around food sources. Groups would settle near the source and gather around fire to survive. These survival tactics helped form social norms. Information was shared verbally, in song, or in simple writings, and decisions were made. Connections were direct, person-to-person. They were seamless. The Connected World, at its core, is the same today as it was back then, which is about connecting people and driving value. The simple model of connecting people is seen in figure 1.

Figure 1 – Information Flow Has Traditionally Been between and for People.

As time passed, the world further developed and grew more complex. Many "things" were introduced. Tools, consumer goods, and devices entered our lives. Stores, homes, restaurants, parks, and entertainment venues were introduced as places consumers lived and operated. Each of these settings contained additional things in them that added some sort of value to a consumer's life. Consumers also needed ways to move between these places, so eventually bikes, cars, buses, planes, and boats emerged, introducing diverse ways to transport people and their personal goods. As society continued to mature and populations grew, specialties emerged in the working class, as did specialty tools. Similarly, business-oriented complexities became a common occurrence. Factories, office buildings, warehouses, roadways, hospitals, as well as freight trains, semitrucks, and cargo boats and planes all emerged into the common landscape of a business ecosystem. Look out your window. We live in a complex world. People and things are interacting throughout the day, every day. The things used in and around our lives inform our experiences. See figure 2 for a simplified graphical representation of our world that is connecting. The people are still in the picture; however, now information flows from, to, and through a much more complex ecosystem. This is our landscape for our Connected World.

Figure 2 – Things and People Interacting and Exchanging Information.

What has remained constant is the need for and recognized value in trading information between people. This communication must now account for these things. This added layer of communication between things can either add value to people's lives or steal value from it. Adding value often requires the things to fit into the ecosystem seamlessly. Until the advent of IoT, it was always the responsibility of the person to ensure this integration took place. Connected products now allow for products to work with one another in a more relevant way. This relevancy may change the way a product works. It may even change the way the product is priced or consumed and how a service is administered or consumed.

Consider our CEO friend Manuel's connected fork. In today's world, eating lunch would rarely impact how a ride to a soccer game should be scheduled. In the Connected World, internet-enabled products can offer information that logically links disparate parts of a day or different parts of a life. Although complex, the Connected World is one full of promise for the people. If done well, information will flow and make experiences as seamless as they were around a campfire thousands of years ago. A perfectly refined Connected World is one where the stakeholder's journey is both informed and integrated, which will allow him to earn back the most valuable commodity: time.

It's imperative leaders remember that the Connected World is about the people who live in it, and not just the machines and data enabling it. Leaders working on IoT too often put the product they will connect in the center of the conversation. We have seen many leaders from product companies literally make graphics that represent their connected strategy and place their "connected thing" in the middle with all of the other devices, processes, and people attached to it. Installing sensors in an inferior product and connecting it is not the key to competing in the Connected World. Product utility is still necessary, even if it is insufficient. Leaders need to consider a more design-centric view and put the human (e.g., user, customer, etc.) in the center of the strategy. Maintaining the traditional product-centric view of the world leaves the work of integrating the experience—exchanging information with other parts of the network to create contextual value—to the user. This process has always worked because people are in the habit of integrating both technological and nontechnical information. If someone is driving, for example, she will have to integrate road signs and the other vehicles on the road. She will have to type the address of her destination into the navigation system and open the garage door when she arrives home. It also falls on today's driver to check that she has valid insurance and enough fuel, and that a different family member is not using the car. The user, in other words, is responsible for making sure everything works together and within the context for any particular trip.

As more and more things move online, however, the single connected product your company offers becomes one of many things that will inform a specific experience for the user. A driver or rider will have a multitude of connected things that will play a role in her experience of driving: the connected car itself, which includes the navigation and entertainment systems, the passengers' preferences and schedules, the connected home, and charging station availability are just some examples. This integration responsibility is not just in the car but also in the home, in the store, in the workplace. Everywhere. The profusion of connected products and services will eventually become overwhelming. There will be too many connections and too much data for her to control and manage. People will lose the ability to act as master integrators. This isn't to suggest they'll become Luddites. Rather, the expectations of consumers will evolve. They will begin demanding that businesses provide seamless integration for the products and services they offer.

In the Connected World, your customers will abandon a product the moment they feel it has become too difficult to integrate. It's crucial, therefore, for you to factor in the issue of integration when designing products, creating business models, and forging business relationships. All of your actions should be based on the following under-standing: the Connected World is one that removes the human from the role of integrator between two services, two products, or a product and a service. The integration should automatically occur for the person's benefit.

If the future is one where every meaningful device in the consumer's life will be connected, then unconnected products will not have the same value to a user as ones that are part of a larger ecosystem. Unconnected products will only be used in special situations. Some may find a way into a collector's item category, such as antiques or craft works. Others may be a commodity item where human integration is easy and deemed appropriate. Often, we ask our students to give examples of items that will never be logically connected. The year 2017 was the first time when students couldn't imagine a product not connected. Prior to this, there were always some students arguing that a screw, clothing, or cleaning solution wouldn't be connected. We have reached a tipping point of recognition that most products, if connected to a broader ecosystem, will bring value to the user. As you will read in future chapters, this value may come directly to the user, to the user through the added value in the ecosystem, or to the manufacturer and passed back to the user in price or services. As long as IoT technology and information are passed on for the people, we are on the way to a very Connected World.

REAL TRANSFORMATION IS REQUIRED

Often, when companies set a course to compete in the connecting world, they don't look far enough down the runway. They don't see potential disruption to the industry. They end up stopping short of completing the necessary transformation. Maybe they'll connect the next generation of the product but make connectivity a premium option, instead of core to their new business model. They may buy the capabilities to deliver a connected service for today, instead of redesigning their company so that it's ready to compete in tomorrow's more advanced Connected World.

A car company, for example, isn't transforming from an automotive company to a mobility company if only one percent of its vehicles in operation are connected. This doesn't reshape the business and its accompanying capabilities. An appliance company is not transforming its company to participate in the multiple revenue streams if only some of its appliances connect to help monitor usage, sense needed repairs, or become part of the supply chain for groceries or laundry detergent. One-off connected features are baby steps, insufficient to get the company where it needs to go in order to stay competitive in the Connected World. Inexperienced product managers may feel good to claim a connected strategy in motion if they have launched a sales app, or a stand-alone connected feature, but leaders need to look much deeper. For a complete transformation to take place, leaders must fully understand the Connected World as a technological discontinuity.

It's not easy to shed the past and become the future, but that's exactly what needs to happen. It's why we wrote this book. You're leading your organization during a time of tremendous change. Disruption at the industry level will necessitate the transformation of firms. It will force you to lead differently. But it's a change that will offer fantastic opportunity.

Understand that a threat to your company and its position in its industry emerges due to advent of this *technological discontinuity*, which is when a new emergent technology offers highly superior benefits over an existing technology. The new technology, which sometimes stands on the shoulders of the previous one, breaks the preceding technology's dominance. This technological discontinuity drives the need to consider new strategies, which often require new capabilities. These shifts in strategy and capabilities will force the need for *organizational transformation*. The process and speed of obtaining these new capabilities is never homogeneous. Some companies are faster than others when it comes to shifting the business model. Other companies may move quickly, but in an effort to try to predict the future, they make the wrong choices. Differences in efficacy and speed of reaction lead to *industry disruption*. Companies that operate with the highest inertia and are unable to take the steps to adjust to the technological discontinuity will fail. The reality is that some companies will go out of business, or be consumed wholly or in part by an adjacent competitor. The quicker your company manages to understand the disruption and adapt to the technological discontinuity, the greater its chances of defending and increasing market share. Hopefully, when the new hierarchy in the industry reestablishes itself, you'll find your company in a better position.

This path from technological discontinuity to industry disruption is highly predictable. We have lived, studied, and taught it, and advised others on how to face it for many years. The result of our work is a simple model (see figure 3) that can guide your thinking as you move your company forward. We will further explore this model throughout this book to better understand how to navigate the pattern of industry disruption (base row), company transformation (middle row), and the executive leader's process to get started (top row).

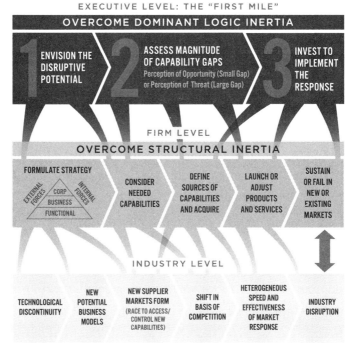

Figure 3 – CGS Advisors Core Transformation Framework

In the chapters that follow, we will act as your guides through this framework that will help you prepare to lead during this time of change. It's the same model we've used with countless firms undergoing similar challenges. For many years, we have taught our MBA students and coached our corporate executive clients from *Fortune* 500 and midsized companies with the same model. We now present this solution in what we hope is an engaging, thought-provoking text.

First, you'll explore how technological discontinuities lead to industry disruption, and how the technologies that are leading to the connecting world have been building on one another for some time. We will then turn to the economic models that are emerging as products connect and services emerge, with businesses built around these technologies. This backdrop will allow you as the leader to build perspective for how your industry, and more importantly your firm, can compete in this impending future.

The aircraft jet engine industry is an example of how a technological discontinuity disrupts a stable industry. Perhaps, historically, the number one and two companies in the industry, in terms of market share, had long been settled. Two other companies were constantly jockeying for the third and fourth positions. Then IoT came along, and the jet engine's embedded sensors now provided a steady stream of precise data to the airplane operators and manufacturers regarding usage, productivity, and the condition of the equipment.

This technology forced industry leaders to rethink what business they were in. Were they still selling jet engines, or were they now selling a data-enabled service? Some companies invested resources into identifying the value of the information produced by these sensors. With this knowledge, they redrafted their business models, adjusted their capabilities, and formed partnerships with companies that could add value to the data. In fact, some changed what they were selling altogether. Instead of selling jet engines, they sold "guaranteed engine output." Other companies were aware of the data collected by the sensors but could not imagine how it impacted their core business of selling heavy machinery.

The company that was previously bouncing between the third and fourth position was the first to come to market with a service that provided up-to-the-second information on the health of the machines, saving businesses from downtime in their facilities. In a short time, this company found itself with the largest market share. The industry leader embedded several sensors into its products, but it was a perfunctory move. Eventually, the company lost the ability to compete and sales dropped dramatically. This former industry leader became a sub-component supplier for the former number two, which slowly retooled and found itself bouncing between the second and third positions.

With this perspective, we will help you, the leader, walk through a critical three-step process. First, we will guide you to gain perspective on the market-facing challenges that will confront companies in the Connected World. If you plan on staying relevant, it's vital to appreciate the unique ecosystems this world will create. It's not only a question of what your product or service will specifically offer users, but also the other companies and industries that will contribute to the rest of the user's experience. What products or services are engaged prior to using your products? How does your firm's product relate to these other services the consumer is using? Are there other products or services used in conjunction with your product? What products are engaged after the use of your product?

The answers to the above questions are the greatest signifiers of a product's value in the Connected World. Once the ecosystem is charted, your firm can begin exchanging data with other companies in the ecosystem with the goal of providing a more autonomous, seamless, and comfortable experience for the user. The quicker you manage to embed your company in the emerging ecosystem, the more likely it is the business will survive, because it's much harder to find an open spot once the structure is in place.

With this perspective, the next guided step will be to shape your strategies at the corporate, business, and functional levels. You'll need to understand how industry lines are blurring and how suppliers are displacing OEMs from end customers. These industry-level changes will help inform what business you wish to be in and formally define your corporate strategy. Then you'll need to look inward and understand where your strengths are, and how you can leverage them to compete in this new business. This will form the basis of your business strategy. Last, you'll need to consider your resourcing and define your functional strategies.

Your strategy will only be realized if your firm has the right capabilities to execute against it. We will work to explore the capabilities needed in the connecting world, whether it's those you already have and need to exploit, or ones you need to obtain. We will consider sourcing strategies, and provide you with considerations of how to address your gaps.

Additionally, we will help you anticipate the pitfalls your firm may encounter in managing change. It's one thing to develop a sound plan, and another to execute against it. Do you have unrecognized sources of organizational inertia that will slow the transformation at the moment you're ready to accelerate for the change? The vast majority of products and services, as of now, are either not connected or haven't been provided with meaningful connections. Many business leaders are playing a waiting game, pushing off making changes until they have a firmer idea of how this world will look. It's our hope that by reading this book you'll understand that industry disruption caused by technological discontinuity will occur during your career. For better or worse, the Connected World will leave its mark on every type of company and industry.

You, and all business leaders, are going down a dangerous road if you're approving products, budgets, or basic expenditures under the assumption that you're still dealing with discrete products or finite services in an insulated industry. Failing to prepare for this shift means you won't participate in the Connected World and won't capture the future value of customers using your products.

Finally, we will encourage you to be brave and lead your company into the connected future. Don't be the CEO who one day looks around the office wondering when the point of total connectivity arrived and what this may mean for your product. For many CEOs, it's an ongoing source of dissonance. They're focused more on performance, less on actual value, and what a current industry demands, instead of the capabilities their firm will need to compete in the future. The signs of what's coming are all around us, if only we'd open our eyes.

This book will work as a guide as you begin to plan for finding your company's place in a future ecosystem. It's an important read if you're a business leader who sees the coming change and wants to know how the Connected World will be different and what capabilities your companies will need to acquire in order to meet the challenge. More importantly, this book is a wake-up call to anyone who hasn't yet either considered or accepted the coming discontinuity. Taking the initial steps to reshape your company's capabilities one month, quarter, or year before the competition can mean the difference between ruin and survival.

WHO WE ARE

Greggory R. Garrett is the founder and CEO of CGS Advisors, LLC, a boutique strategic transformation and innovation advisory firm serving clients globally. He has always pushed the limits of cultures by formulating and implementing unique market-disrupting strategies. An accomplished leader, Gregg takes pride in recognizing commonsense solutions for complex and systemic problems and supports "corporate bravery" by motivating teams to reach well beyond the typical boundaries in order to achieve greatness.

Recognizing the complexity of emerging macroeconomic ecosystems, Gregg has recently led the launch of Connected Detroit Innovates, a cross-industry consortium of chief innovation officers who are committed to collaborating in an effort to succeed in the Connected World.

Gregg's academic training, rooted in systems engineering, was enhanced with an MBA focused in integrative management. He spent close to a decade as a consultant at Ernst & Young before moving to leadership positions at Volkswagen and Deutsche Telekom. In his last role before founding CGS Advisors, Gregg was the chief strategy officer for IT and innovation at Volkswagen in North America, where he developed and led the digital strategy and innovation practice for one of the largest automotive companies in the world.

Throughout his twenty-five-plus years in product, telecom, IT, and advisory services industries, Gregg has been occupied with the questions and challenges surrounding change and transformation. In the beginning of his career, he was identified as a problem solver. After years of studying crises and predicaments, he developed an eye for identifying systemic opportunities before they emerged.

Gregg is a "maker." He founded his first firm at the age of sixteen, a collegiate lacrosse program by twenty, and his first industry consortium by twenty-nine. Gregg is also a teacher. He has coauthored a Harvard Business School case, keynoted and spoken at more than fifty global conferences, and is an adjunct faculty and lecturer at several business and engineering schools. As a leader, Gregg sits on several corporate advisor boards, chaired a not-for-profit association, and has been coaching since he was fourteen.

Gregg's unique blend of professional management experiences in corporate settings, entrepreneurism, systemic understanding of enterprises, and knowledge of upcoming technologies makes him passionate about two distinct areas:

- The Connected World: The evolving ultraconnected environment of people AND products will revolutionize the world economy over the next ten years.
- People: The best strategies are useless unless people are motivated to understand and implement them.

Gregg is a dedicated father to two sons, and the husband to his wife, Amy, who continuously encourages him to live life with no regrets.

Dr. Warren Ritchie, after more than thirty-five years of work is moving progressively and deliberately into retirement, stepping away from the internal bustle of organizations. He intends to continue with advisory projects where the involved people are passionate and the issues interesting.

Warren has worked in the public sector, academia, and the private sector in civil aviation, technology, and automotive industries. He has accumulated bachelor's, master's, and doctoral degrees from universities in Canada and the United States. Warren has taken roles across multiple functional areas including sales, marketing, finance, supply chain, strategy, and IT. During his years in corporations, he rose to C-level executive roles in multiple functional areas.

Post the corporate world, Warren became an independent business consultant who contributed to the start-up of CGS Advisors and was the CGS practice leader for strategy services. He continues to contribute through the CGS Fellows Program.

His next goal is to perfect the double haul cast and explore some of the saltwater flats of the world.

The two authors began collaborating in 2002 when Gregg joined a Volkswagen Group consulting services company and partnered with Warren, who was responsible for a massive corporate strategy initiative that included the transformation of the IT function. They quickly discovered that their unique viewpoints on how companies transform in disrupted industries played off each other to exceptional results. The partnership blossomed as they carried their transformation program globally through

North and South America and eventually Europe. In 2008, the partnership deepened when Warren, who was then the CIO, brought over Gregg to become the head of strategy and innovation. Four years later, they operationalized Corporate Growth Strategy (CGS) Advisors, a boutique strategy and innovation firm whose chief focus is helping businesses prepare for industry disruption caused by emerging technologies. CGS Advisors supports companies as they identify unique paths to growth and facilitate internal transformations so they can stay competitive in the Connected World. This book aims to share the authors' experiences, knowledge, and approach with a broad group of leaders that may not have direct access to their boutique advisory firm.

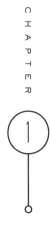

THE BUSINESS OF THE CONNECTED WORLD

"The immutable force of competition is already engaged, it will not stop. Will you be ready?"

TECHNOLOGICAL DISCONTINUITY LEADS TO INDUSTRY DISRUPTION

Throughout history, discoveries and technological advancements have reshaped society and how people live. When a technology emerges, it soon enters the adaptation process. People will work to try to determine its functional utility. If it's deemed to have no or limited value, then it will be cast aside. If, however, it's determined to carry a unique and greater value, it will soon become the prevailing standard—until a newer technology materializes, one that builds on the previous technology's functionality and value.

As technology evolves, companies and industries will follow. In this timeless model, known as technological discontinuity, a new and superior technology displaces a legacy technology that has become embedded in an industry. The new emergent technology offers highly superior benefits over the existing technology, which "discontinues" the dominance of the previous technology. The technological discontinuity encourages people to think about commercial applications and whether the innovation allows them to apply the technology to differentiate their offering to the market. Once meaningful differentiation is identified, companies must immediately consider the capabilities required to pursue this model. This forces them to consider how they will acquire these capabilities. Firms may or may not use a methodical process to answer the above questions, and each company does so at a different pace. Some will ask these questions and attempt to find solutions earlier than others. Also, the capabilities of certain companies are well positioned to swiftly move toward the opportunity. Firms lacking the capabilities will have a much longer road. Organizations that are able to move faster in an effective manner can improve their standing in the industry. The same holds true for new entrants, who don't enter the industry with as many constraints. What we have just described is a process that has repeated itself over history. It is captured in figure 4.

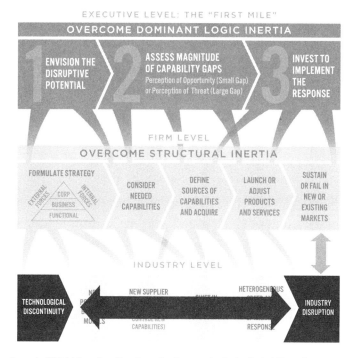

Figure 4 – CGS Advisors Core Transformation Framework – Technological Discontinuity Leads to Industry Disruption.

THE PAST WILL FORECAST THE FUTURE

The Connected World is not the first instance of techno-logical discontinuity. Human society has lived through many of these periods, and if you look around your day-to-day life, you will see examples of results of prior moments of technological discontinuity. When you turn on a lamp, you are experiencing the results of electrical power generation and distribution that ended the era of candle power. When you drive in your car, you are experiencing the combustion engine that ended the era of the horse.

The steam engine, although not often personally experienced, is a technology that had a significant impact on many industries and even entire nations. Imagine you were a mill owner in the 1700s, when the first steam engine was invented. You wouldn't have had the luxury of celebrating this wondrous invention. The other firms in the industry would've been busy identifying various opportunities and challenges the technology presented to your business. Once you and your competitors identified these commercial opportunities and threats, the real work of substituting this new technology for the flowing water you were currently using to power your mill would have already begun. It wasn't a matter of simply plugging in a new technology. Using this artificially created power source required the acquisition of an entire set of new and modified capabilities and changes to the strategy. For instance, thanks to this invention, you'd no longer be required to establish your mill next to a flowing body of water. You'd have the option to relocate to a more favorable location, such as close to new clients or adjacent to the source of raw materials. There'd also be the opportunity to invest in steam-powered machinery, which would boost productivity. Workers who were skilled in containing and regulating the steam so there wouldn't be explosions would become crucial. Learning the technologies surrounding keeping the boiler hot will become another requirement. Exploiting this new technology, in other words, would necessitate time, trial, and error. Speed would've been a crucial element. Perhaps the discoverers of the innovation had already bought an existing mill and were retrofitting it with the latest technology, putting them in a prime position to lead the reshaped industry.

These opportunities to get ahead of the curve present themselves with every major technological breakthrough. Obviously, you want to make these decisions as close as possible to the beginning of the technology's emergence, getting a head start on the competition, which is already responding to the discontinuity. Human curiosity is timeless, and so is striving to push the boundaries of what's possible and reach new heights. It takes significant amounts of intellect and resources to see a technology's potential, understand the challenges and opportunities, and do what's necessary to build a workable model and compete. These attributes of curiosity, endeavoring, and intellect aren't equally distributed throughout the population, which is why some firms will come out ahead, while others will fall away. There's also a significant middle ground, where many organizations will eventually obtain the capabilities and find a place in the industry's new hierarchy.

We can apply this broad pattern to the Connected World,

which is the discontinuity of today. The current technological discontinuity, the Connected World, is a phenomenon of the evolution in computing over the last eighty years. Understanding how this technology has evolved can further help us appreciate how the wide-ranging societal implications of technological discontinuity can lead to a swift and massive restructuring of known industry hierarchy and the potential creation of new industries. The evolution that is summarized in figure 5 shows how each computing era has had different disruptive potential that builds on the prior technological innovation.

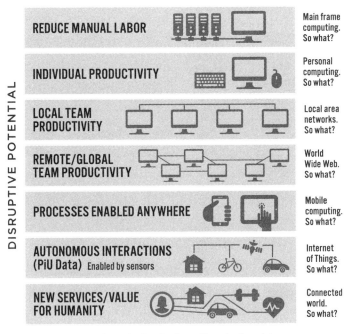

Figure 5 – Progression of Computing Eras Leading to Disruptive Potential.

Major advancements in pre-silicon and silicon-based technologies brought mainframe computers to businesses in the late 1940s and early 1950s. These machines, which lacked an interactive component, took up entire rooms in offices, allowing for the automation and centralization of traditionally manual tasks, such as payroll and customer billing. Due to the size and cost, mainframes affected only the largest firms by allowing for the processing of manual calculations at scale. This increased productivity resulted in the redundancy of capabilities, which could be retired. Of course, in order to gain these efficiencies, these firms required new capabilities in the form of specialists to work the mainframes and extract the produced information.

Over time, the miniaturization of integrated circuits and processing meant the processing power of the mainframe could now be shifted to the desktop, and even more functions could be automated. Large monitors replaced inboxes and folders on the desks of workers.

Additional change was felt when companies were able to link individual computers together and create a local network. Workers were now able to share files, enhancing the value of the desktop computer and leading to even greater productivity. Soon, these internal networks were able to connect to outside networks. Eventually, a standard protocol was created to help disparate computers speak with one another across many networks, and the internet was born. This development brought about not only greater productivity but also greater access to knowledge. Answers and solutions to almost any problem were now easily attainable. From this point forward, technology reoriented itself to the question of how to gain wider and faster access to information.

Computer processing power miniaturized further, networks went wireless, and mobile computing materialized as the next technological disruption. Thanks to laptops, smartphones, tablets, and phablets, people no longer had to stay tethered to their desktop computers if they wanted to work productively, shop, be entertained, or generally have access to information. The ability to log on to the internet while on the go gave people more time and opportunities to tackle other work and personal responsibilities. A new value, the internet's social media feature, emerged during this phase.

Mobile technologies and embedded sensors enabled our current phase of the Internet of Things (IoT), where information is autonomously exchanged between devices and networks. The collected data in the IoT doesn't necessarily surface in the form of a human-centered service, but this will change in the Connected World, where the value of the information will flow from sensors in devices and clearly inform value for humans. Companies will use the data to design services that seamlessly integrate into a network of other services and products already utilized by the consumer, employee, or citizen.

Every stage of advancement in computing technology laid the foundation for the next one that would emerge, bringing with it increased utility and greater value. Consequently, the disruptions became more pronounced with each shift as they diffused through organizations and societies. Mainframe computers disrupted accounting departments in offices, and employees had to be brought on to operate the machines; yet, they had a negligible disruptive effect on society at large. The personal desktop, however, disrupted the workflow of almost every employee in an office, which meant more of society was impacted. As the internet took off, companies began selling goods online, which not only completely altered business models but also changed the daily habits of ordinary people. Mobile networks meant productivity and convenience could be taken anywhere. As computers were integrated into other machines, more complex problems could be automated, and systems of systems could emerge with value being recognized on an exponential scale.

TODAY'S DISCONTINUITY: THE TIME IS NOW

This computing and information technology transition from mainframes to personal computers to internet-enabled mobile devices occurred over the course of many decades. The shift into IoT and the Connected World and its ripple effect on all industries, however, is happening much faster. Soon, consumers will appreciate the immense difference in value between a thing that is connected and one that is not.

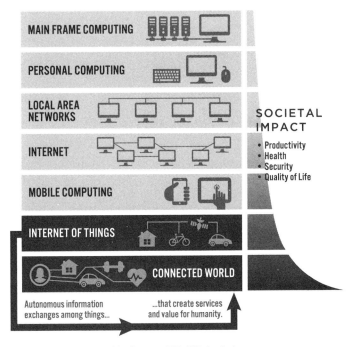

Figure 6 – Additive Impact of the Connected World Technologies.

As more things connect and more sources of data continue to expand, value will be understood differently, and ecosystems will begin to take shape in order to process, multiply, and distribute the value. Individuals, groups of people, and entire societies will become more dependent on these ecosystems in order to improve productivity, health, security, and even their overall quality of life. As seen in figure 6, this is how our Connected World will create true services of value for users and humans. As these ecosystems form, users will be forced to integrate unconnected products. This added effort may become tiresome as more and more autonomous information ecosystems emerge. Unconnected products, therefore, will have less value to consumers as an isolated product. At best, they will become a curiosity for collectors or specialists, much like vinyl records or the rotary phone.

Companies will only succeed in getting their products and services into potential customers' hands if their offering effortlessly integrates into the other technologies the person is currently using. These companies will have to go to the customers, and not the other way around.

Once things are connected, the data and services they produce will account for more than fifty percent of the product's value, essentially marking the end, or the discontinuation, of the era of discrete, unconnected things.

The ability to take advantage of this change in how users evaluate products will be unequally distributed across industries. Some firms will adapt faster to the new reality. Other firms will manage to change in meaningful ways, as opposed to adding new connected functions that prove worthless. New entrants will take advantage of the low cost of entry and rapidly gain market share. In the end, these companies will gain industry prominence at the expense of former powerhouses.

CONTINUING CONFLUENCE AND EXTENSIONS OF THE CONNECTED WORLD

The confluence of technologies that will make the Connected World possible shows no signs of stopping. New tributaries of technological disruptions are constantly flowing into the current landscape, and emerging technologies that will discontinue the connectivity in this world are just over the horizon. Virtual reality, augmented reality, and mixed reality. Machine learning and artificial intelligence. Kinematics and digital bots. These are just some of the most recent examples for the connecting world that help cement the effects on business and society. Each one will carry its own diffusion model and disruptive potential and, like previous computing technology eras, will also build on one another in our ultimate Connected World.

Shorter cycle times mean you will not have the luxury of waiting for a trend to establish itself before deciding how to act. Industry stability used to be measured in decades, whereas now, it's calculated in years. This makes it impossible to sit out a cycle and insert your company at a later date. If you don't start shifting on a structural level and thinking about information and experience-driven models, taking the human out of the integration role, then you will miss your chance to embrace these technologies as opportunities, and they will instead become threats.

In addition to the technologies that signal a deepening of the Connected World, other movements may prove equally disruptive. As technology becomes embedded, we've witnessed the rise of a computer-era-maker movement, where people at home tinker with these technologies to extend beyond the original commercially available options. Advances in 3-D and 4-D printing will bring massive disruption to manufacturing. Other industries should expect to see a spillover effect. All products will see changes similar to the ones seen in mobile phones. Multi-use platforms, in other words, will become standard for many products.

WE HAVE REACHED THE TIPPING POINT

"Why now?" This is a common question as leaders consider how they must react to the connecting world. Just a few years ago, the Connected World was not logical. It couldn't be understood or envisioned. Now, however, the visions of the future like we laid out in the introduction are believable. They are not science fiction. What is still often wondered is why it is happening now. After all, technology has continued to change for decades. What makes this era so much more disruptive than those that preceded it?

The basic components of the Connected World, as depicted in figure 7, are rather simple.

Figure 7 – Simple Components of the Connected World.

"Why now?" Because all the elements of the Connected World have been built out and are readily available. The computing technology elements are the results of the computing eras previously discussed:

- Ubiquitous Networks: For many decades incredible capital investments have been made to connect high-speed long-range networks, both wired and wireless, across the globe. Coupled with the advancement in recent years of short-range networking standardization (e.g., Bluetooth), most products and solutions can be effectively connected to one another or to a central computing center.
- Embedded Technology: Moore's law has continued to be proven correct. Computer processing and storage is small enough, fast enough, and cheap enough to be put in almost all devices.
- The Cloud: What doesn't make sense to embed into a device can now be easily provisioned in a data center. Data centers were once huge capital expenditures by the company that wanted to offer the solutions. Now

"cloud providers" offer computing processing and storage on a pay-as-you-go model.

- Mobile Consumer Devices: In much of the world, we carry mini computers with internet connections and dozens of sensors around in our pockets. Today's smartphone is packed with so much technology that can often be "borrowed" as part of a connected solution or offering. When you download an app, you're likely authorizing the producer of that app to use your processor, your screen, your internet connection, and sensors inside your phone.

- You, We, or Us: Over the last ten years, many people have grown accustomed to sharing information via social channels. We've learned to trade data for value. This societal shift enables new business models in the Connected World.

All these developments ease entry into the Connected World. Many of the architectural elements that render a product or service connected no longer require a new entrant to bring a large capital investment. A company can piggyback on the technologies of existing products with ease. The cell phone every person carries in his or her pocket or bag, with its already embedded sensors, is the clearest example. Networks and cloud computing, other key aspects of the Connected World, are also already in place. Technically, there's very little to stop companies from connecting every product.

Take, for instance, the "connected wine bottle." It may trigger images of wine producers attaching screens and cellular connections to each bottle to market and track the product. If this were the case, no matter the quality of the wine, they'd need to sell each bottle for hundreds of dollars in order to offset the cost of the technology. What a low barrier to entry means is that wine producers can connect their products by sticking behind the bottle's label an NFC (near-field communication) chip, which is a small circuit board that has no active connectivity. A consumer browsing the shelves at a wine store can place her cell phone against the label. The phone's power activates the chip, and then the phone's processor and network connection are used to communicate with the "cloud." It might also borrow sensor information (e.g., GPS information, temperature, etc.) to customize the information it receives from the cloud. Eventually, the phone's screen is used to tell the consumer about the bottle of wine in front of her. It may tell the story of the grapes and the wine's production, or suggest decanting instructions, pairings, and information on the winery's other offerings. In essence, the wine producer, distributor, and retailer are counting on the connected consumer to participate in turning a stand-alone bottle of wine into a connected product that controls messaging, reports status, and may build a differentiated experience.

This easy access to technology is why the pace of transition into this next stage is accelerating. An individual or small team of college students can imagine a great idea for a service and use the investments of large companies and the customer population to enable the system. No large capital investments or long build times are required. They likely don't need to be mechanical engineers or computer scientists to get their ideas off the ground either. Affordable freelance programmers, engineers, and graphic designers can be found on the internet on a pay-per-job basis. The students can rent space on an already existing cloud and can also assume that the eventual user will supply the connectivity and power. Conceptual integration is the only thing that's required of them. The world in which we compete is truly connecting!

INDUSTRY DISRUPTION IS INEVITABLE

Technological discontinuities disrupt industry. There is no doubt that the technological platforms that are enabling the Connected World will follow the same pattern. An industry is disrupted when a new hierarchy of prominence of firms is dramatically different from before the effects of discontinuity (as seen in figure 8).

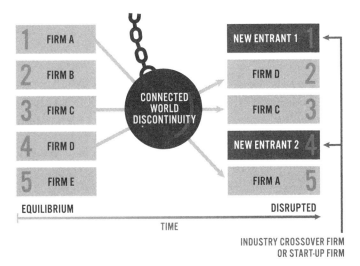

Figure 8 – Graphical Representation of Industry Disruption.

Several different firm movements can influence this new prominence mix:

- New Entrants: The entry of new entrants can occur when new firms (i.e., start-ups) choose to enter a market, or when established firms pivot into a new market (i.e., industry crossover).
- Current Industry Shifts: Firms will react to the Connected World at different speeds, and some will capitalize and rise in prominence, while others will lag and fall in prominence.
- Consolidation: Other firms may combine to compete as the industry dynamics shift.
- Exit: In the end, some firms will fail. Typically, these are slow "deaths."

In the end, leaders need to anticipate that their industries will be disrupted and their firm's prominence will change due to this rapidly emerging technical discontinuity. There is no stopping it, yet it's critical to recognize when an industry- (and cross-industry-) level disruption is occurring so leaders can understand the type of decisions necessary for their firm.

RECOGNIZING THE PATTERNS OF DISCONTINUITY

There's no doubt that the shift into the Connected World will bring radical, rapid changes to the business landscape. Looking at the patterns of discontinuity to disruption, it's clear leaders cannot reinvent how technological discontinuity will act as a disrupting force on businesses and society. Suggesting that discontinuity will not impact a firm or lead to industry disruption is foolish. In many ways, most firms are already being impacted.

The Connected World is, in fact, the latest stage in a pattern that started in the late 1940s with the development of mainframe computers. Appreciate that the technologies making up this new world are evergreen technologies. They're built on the preceding technologies, and they'll be the forerunners of the next great breakthroughs. Connectivity is coming to every device that surrounds us. Data will inform the product and service experiences companies provide. Now is the time to prepare for this outcome.

Otherwise, you risk becoming the millwork owner who decided to keep his mill next to the river, the one who lost his position in the industry when he encountered disadvantages such as greater labor and transportation costs.

Technological advances come in all forms and sizes. Sometimes they're barely noticeable, while other times they upend entire economies. Some build on prior technologies, and other discoveries provide novel ways of looking at problems. The human element, however, is the one constant. Progress, no matter the degree, stems from the evergreen force of curiosity and ambition. A constant desire to improve life fuels humans. Their days are spent exploring, discovering, and creating things of value. Yet, breakthroughs themselves aren't enough to alter the world. The major leaps happen only when people can envision how the new technology will enhance people's lives.

In organizations, it takes special leaders to recognize the potential of innovative technologies to add value to products. They not only can visualize how the commercial possibilities will transform their business models but also possess a willingness to see how their companies may have to start competing in other industries. These are the leaders who will trigger positive transformations for their organizations. They're the mill owners who left the competition behind when they picked up and moved to the major cities.

Speed of recognition makes successful adaptation to the new technology heterogeneous among firms. The faster a leader understands a technology's value and potential for disruption, the quicker he or she will be to execute changes. Leaders must choose if they will position their firm as a first mover (i.e., early adopter), become a laggard, or fight for resources with the majority of companies transforming.

INTEGRATION MATURITY LEADS TO DISRUPTION IN THE CONNECTED WORLD

The technologies leading to the Connected World have the power to disrupt across multiple industries. Because data, at its core, powers this discontinuity, its value can span widely beyond typical industry boundaries. This is why innovation in the Connected World is occurring at the fringe of traditional industries. Information from nonfamiliar places is beginning to inform product and service experiences, and "frictionless experiences" are becoming the focus for product managers and marketers alike.

Discrete industry classifications will no longer be sufficient in this world. We are entering an era of ecosystems, which is grounded in the idea of massive integration at various levels. These levels are captured in a logical progression model in figure 9.

PROGRESSION OF INTEGRATION IN THE CONNECTED ERA

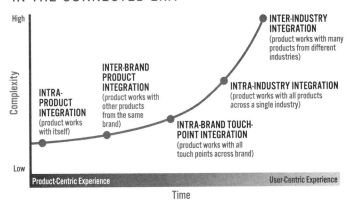

Figure 9 – Progression of Integration in the Connected World.

As more firms move through these phases of connected integration and products take on more and more of a platform feel, distinct product categories will disappear, making disruption more easily recognizable. Today's industry types will likely continue to shift support-adjusted ecosystems and new value chains. These changes will occur at different speeds for each firm and industry segment.

Currently, we find ourselves earlier in this progression, primarily being informed from a "product-centric" perspective. Even though products are now connecting, the term "IoT" is still a good description of the current state of affairs. Firms are concentrating first on bringing the Internet industries together with the Things industry. With this type of connection, the product works with itself, making it the most basic type of connectivity. Referred to as intra-product integration, this type of integration forms the basis of all types of products, whether it's a car, airplane, or television. The subcomponents of a vehicle must all work together to ensure it gives a relevant function-based experience, which would be moving from point A to point B.

Leaders need to appreciate that in the connected era, customers won't accept products that are connected for a single feature. They will also demand inter-brand-product integration, which is when a product works with other products from the same brand. Information flows seamlessly between all the products in a company's portfolio. Apple is an example of a company that has succeeded in creating a uniform experience for customers. Its products all operate in an identical manner, and information flows freely between devices. Users can put down one device and continue working on a second device without having to manually transfer data.

Intra-brand touch-point integration is the most sophisticated type of connectivity companies are achieving in the IoT. In this level of connectivity, all the touch points across the brand—the call center, website, mobile app, and product itself—are integrated. Another term for this is "omnichannel." The customer is in constant contact with the company through a wide variety of channels. If the user calls technical support, the operator won't need to ask what product the person is using or how it's being utilized. The operator will be monitoring its use in real time. The product becomes the ultra-customer touch point!

The previous types of connectivity described have been product-centric. They help the customer or user end the need to be the integrator of the experience as it relates to its primary purpose, or within its brand ecosystem. In the Connected World, the connectivity will provide user-centric experience. This is reflected in the next highest level of integration (intra-industry integration) in which products and services work seamlessly across all relevant touch points in a single experience.

A smart thermostat should work seamlessly with all the other devices in the house. It shouldn't be the user's responsibility to figure out how to connect the thermostat to the alarm system so that it turns down the air-conditioning every time the person leaves the house. This kind of connectivity will change our definition of certain industries. An alarm company won't necessarily still be in the security industry. Rather, it may move into something that will be called the home device monitoring industry.

In the highest form of connectivity (inter-industry integration), the product or service works with many products from different industries. It's a deepening of the user-centric experience. Imagine a car in which the steering wheel is constantly measuring the pulse of the driver. This real-time data feeds into the driver's health record. A driver may go years without any awareness of this feature, until one day he or she visits the doctor, who reports a recently discovered abnormality in a biometric reading.

All in all, connected consumers are quickly beginning to question why they must play the role of integrator. As products connect and get more complex, they're looking to the product manager to take on this responsibility. Take the car insurance industry, for example. It's been providing IoT devices to plug into a vehicle for many years. Customers must sign up for the service, receive a connected device, and install it in the OBDII port under their steering column. As more and more cars connect, why shouldn't a car automatically report the driver's behavior back to the insurance company? At the same time, the car could provide added value in other areas. The car, for instance, could send a report and its coordinates to the Department of Transportation when its shocks absorb a large pothole, or they could use the connection to pay tolls, carry out emissions testing, and handle registration issues.

Being able to provide this type of complete, seamless experience to drivers will put tremendous pressure on the industry. It will force leaders to stop viewing information as a feature. They'll have to broker agreements with players in other industries in order to create an integrated ecosystem for the drivers of their cars. The consumer will no longer be purchasing a car but instead buying the ability to have an uncomplicated driving or riding experience.

As the level of integration becomes more sophisticated and seamless, the in-use data collected will permeate various layers to create new ecosystems. This will take the Connected World from being a linear phenomenon to an exponential one.

THE TAKEAWAY

Nobody set out to build the architecture of the Connected World. Evolution has been working its magic for more than half a century, putting in place the key infrastructure that allows for this next advance. The inventors of computer mainframes were simply looking for a way to automate and centralize the everyday tasks of offices. All the technological advances of the computer era have developed as a result of addressing specific problems of the time. Embedded technology—cameras, sensors, computing power—was a result of a push into mobile computing. Networks were built to create the internet. Cloud computing was the solution to user-generated data that computers, devices, and IT departments couldn't support.

Cultural changes have also set us up for the Connected

World. People carry a device on them at all times. Sharing information, sometimes unknowingly, is less taboo than in previous eras. People accept the tradeoff of receiving a free app in exchange for their data. They've even come to appreciate how this sharing has the benefit of enhancing present and future experiences. This isn't a top-down model of the government stepping in to build an infrastructure that will meet the demands of a connected future.

Many questions regarding the Connected World remain. We don't know for certain what forms various products and services will take in this new landscape. Uncertainty, however, is a perilous reason for business leaders to wait. By the time there's a clearer picture of where an industry is headed, the disruption will have already occurred, and the new players will have established their spots in the latest iteration of the hierarchy. The only option is to begin preparing at once.

Connecting the product, overhauling your business model, and changing the company's capabilities may feel like an overwhelming undertaking. It's why other leaders will avoid making changes, instead allowing inertia to continue propelling the company's current success. Staying the course feels comfortable. Looking at current market share or dismissing industry start-ups as pie-in-the-sky projects is temporarily reassuring. Meanwhile, the competition is busy figuring out where the industry is headed, which makes it a problematic strategy. These other companies are taking active steps to shift the basis in competition to their advantage.

The sooner you start trying to answer how your products connect to other products and industries, the more you'll see this moment as an opportunity. Alternatively, if you defer thinking about where this is going and deny the need to concretely respond, at some point in the near future, you'll begin to see these changes as a threat. The pieces are already in place. Now is the time to decide whether to act or not.

PREPARE, DON'T PREDICT

"Fortune favors the prepared mind."
—LOUIS PASTEUR

We have suggested that the emergence of the Internet of Things (IoT) might be thought of as the convergence of the Internet (digital) industries and the Things (product) industries. It has been a useful way to begin the discussion about changes in the way firms will compete in the Connected World. Internet industries and product industries, however, have different business practices, which are founded in differences in the economic principles that underlie each industry. We will refer to the economic principles of product industries as "industrial economics" and the economic principles of internet or digital industries as "information economics." In the Connected World, industrial economics and information economics will converge. Further, an economic principle that originated in the industrial era, network effects, will for some businesses act as an accelerator for rapid growth and competitive advantage. The result will be interesting new ways to compete and new business models for companies to adopt. Life will get easier for people using the connected products and services, while life will grow more complicated for executives managing companies hoping to compete.

THE ECONOMIC CONVERGENCE

A story:

An enterprising entrepreneur left his well-paying job in Silicon Valley to open a new bar that would serve the needs of the local technology worker. As he considered all he had learned from his last three positions, he settled on a launch strategy of offering free drinks. During the first month of operations, one million people visited the bar, but not one person paid for a drink. At the end of the month, the entrepreneur announced his high-volume traffic to the venture capital community. Despite a lack of operating revenue, the entrepreneur was now ready to share ownership of his new business and create a seed round offering to qualified investors. He closed the round oversubscribed, prepared to scale his revenue-free business to multiple markets.

The purpose of telling this story is to create an understanding of the contrast in the basis of competition between industrial and information economics. The owner of the bar applied a business practice of information economics—namely, offering a free service (the drinks) to attract and quickly grow a large community of active users of his service (the patrons in the bar). The entrepreneur was attempting to establish a user base without any initial attempt to collect revenue from the users for consuming the service. The launch strategy didn't include revenue. Although the approach seems peculiar in the context of launching a new bar, it's a common practice for digital companies, where the initial digital service offering is not intended to be the revenue source. Rather, its purpose is to create the core asset of the nascent business, which is the user community.

Facebook has the largest community of digital users in the history of the world. It was launched, and continues to operate, without any revenue from the users of the core service. Facebook is, however, a highly profitable firm, deriving its revenue from third-party firms by providing access to its community of users. But Facebook was not always profitable. It took time from the launch of the service until the community was of sufficient size in order to motivate third-party firms to be willing to pay for access. During the time preceding advertising revenue, investors financed Facebook's operation. These investors recognized that Facebook was able to attract regular users. Although it was unclear in the early days whether users would stay with the community and if Facebook would be able to convert them into revenue, investors were willing to commit funds on the potential for profit once the community was established.

The fictitious investors of our new bar in Silicon Valley presumably recognized that growing a community of regular patrons has real value in the world of information economics, even if the means of converting users into a revenue stream has yet to be fully defined.

So why don't real bar businesses launch by offering free drinks for a month to build a user community, and then leverage access to that community to collect revenue? The short answer would be that most new bar owners would go broke, but a more complete answer is in the underlying differences in the economic principles between launching a new bar and a social media service.

First, in a bar every drink is available to be consumed only once, meaning if one customer drinks a glass of beer, that beer is no longer available to be sold again. Another serving of beer is required for the next sale. Each serving of beer costs money for the bar business to purchase. Giving drinks away for free means every drink costs the bar but no revenue is returned. In contrast, each person who joins Facebook and each additional usage have nearly no incremental cost to Facebook. Industrial economics deals with discrete things (servings of beer) and each thing has a cost to create. Information services once appropriately launched, on the other hand, have zero costs for each incremental service user. Adding users to a community in the internet industry is inexpensive, which means growth is low-to-no cost, unlike hard goods industries, which are driven by industrial economics, and each new patron added to a service has an incremental cost.

Second, internet-based services have the ability to monitor the users while they're using the service. In a nonobtrusive way, they can capture and create usage data with every click of a mouse, tap on the screen, or even beat of the heart (e.g., wearables). And this usage data can be informative to the service provider about when, how long, and what features of the digital service are being used, which tells them about both the user and the attractiveness of the service. The usage data for the entire community has potential value to third parties and is the basis for generating future revenue. By contrast, discrete products without sensors don't have any means of collecting usage data and will have considerably less potential value to third parties and limited revenue potential for the product or service provider. When a digital service, such as Facebook, has at its core value the means to create valuable and meaningful interactions among the users, it can, under the right circumstances, create exponential growth in its user base. The larger the community becomes, the more attractive it becomes to remaining non-users, and an upward spiral of user growth ensues, increasing the potential value of the future business with it.

To summarize, digital businesses may launch a service at no charge because it can rapidly grow a community of regular, identifiable users at low cost and easily collect usage data generated by the community that has potential value to third parties. In essence, a digital firm may defer collecting revenue until after it has successfully grown the community. The community can be grown in a "no cost to the user" model, and when it's sustainable, it becomes an asset for the firm, often called an economic or commercial platform. Information economics enable this platform for digital business models. By contrast, for industries offering discrete products, growth of a customer base is not free and there are no efficient ways to create a community of users. Industrial economics business firms are inclined to charge each direct user for each use in advance or as the usage actually occurs.

In figure 10, we show a simple comparison of the various domains of economics to highlight the differences between industrial and information economics.

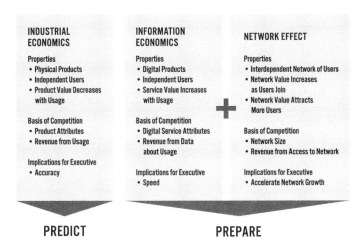

INDUSTRIAL ECONOMICS	INFORMATION ECONOMICS	NETWORK EFFECT
Properties • Physical Products • Independent Users • Product Value Decreases with Usage	**Properties** • Digital Products • Independent Users • Service Value Increases with Usage	**Properties** • Interdependent Network of Users • Network Value Increases as Users Join • Network Value Attracts More Users
Basis of Competition • Product Attributes • Revenue from Usage	**Basis of Competition** • Digital Service Attributes • Revenue from Data about Usage	**Basis of Competition** • Network Size • Revenue from Access to Network
Implications for Executive • Accuracy	**Implications for Executive** • Speed	**Implications for Executive** • Accelerate Network Growth
PREDICT	**PREPARE**	

Figure 10 – Contrast of Industrial and Information Economics.

TODAY'S ECONOMIC PROPERTIES

One of three basic economic principles likely affects the markets in which your firm currently competes: industrial economics, information economics, and network effects. As we move toward the connecting world, the economic principles from each of these areas are colliding, producing a new set of business models. A better understanding of the future Connected World economic principles and business models can be attained when we consider the core of each principle on its own. It's a matter of looking to the past to better understand the future.

INDUSTRIAL ECONOMICS: AN OVERVIEW

Industrial economics deal with discrete products, where

revenue is typically collected when the product is consumed or sold. Furthermore, the value of the product to a user is largely independent of the benefits to any other product owner or user who has purchased the same product. As a general principle of physical products, the value of the product usually declines with usage through wear and tear. In short, with physical products, the more they are used, the less they are worth to the user.

The basis of competition among companies within legacy product industries is in fact largely limited to attributes of the product itself. Firms can differentiate their products on the basis of price, quality, and specialized functionality, all of which are attributes of the product. The product competitors can look to enhance or customize certain services related to the shopping, purchasing, and ownership experiences supporting the product, but these enhancements are largely nuance and unlikely to have a significant effect in determining purchase decisions by consumers. The ability to differentiate on attributes of the product is what sustains product companies. These attributes are typically the largest driver of brand value, which can grow over time as customers see consistency in the way products are offered.

Firms competing in product industries deal with the economic realities of creating physical products. Products are often capital intensive to produce and then have ongoing costs to warehouse and ship each incremental unit before sale. Given the high costs of production, firms typically seek to generate revenue and secure cash flow around the point of consumer usage. Consequently, long-tenured executives in mature product industries are accustomed to the practices related to controlling costs and ensuring that the supply of finished goods available for sale closely matches the demand for the products. Large product firms typically spend considerable effort to forecast future demand with respect to changes in many external variables such as competitor actions, general economic conditions, and social and legal trends.

Legacy product industry executives are typically familiar with reviewing predictions about changes to demand and the potential for increases in costs of doing business. Small changes in demand or internal production costs can represent significant financial risks to the business. The executive's desire for accuracy in decisions drives the need for detailed predictions of external industry change.

For the purposes of this book, we treat legacy, or traditional service firms, as part of the industrial economics paradigm. Taxi companies, lawyers, or doctors are similar to product companies in the sense that they're constrained by a fixed-capacity asset, such as human labor and hours. Information-oriented services companies have a significant difference that must be explored in greater detail.

INFORMATION ECONOMICS: AN OVERVIEW

Digital services best demonstrate the principles of information economics, because the service is not physical in nature and can be offered concurrently to multiple users with minimal increase in the digital service provider's cost. Users can be monitored, and usage patterns can be shared with other users who are simultaneously using or will be using in the future. The usage data has potential value for future revenue, giving digital firms the opportunity for a second revenue stream. This option doesn't exist with product companies. It's the ability of digital companies to capture customer usage data that creates the unique property of digital services in that they increase in value the more they are used.

Further, digital firms often enter their prospective markets as quickly as possible with an initial minimal viable product (MVP) to attract early users. The nature of digital products that are cloud-hosted allows them to be upgraded continuously by the digital company with daily or even hourly releases of new software code to the service. Product firms have no such ability to continually improve the product after it has been purchased.

Digital service firm executives understand that the costs of adding users to the core service is minimal, that the digital service can be continuously enhanced to make the service more attractive, and that the size of the user community enlarges the potential value of usage data. Given all of the above, the economics of information creates the incentives for executives to focus on speedily growing the user community. Detailed internal company analysis of what consumers may prefer is substituted with rapid market trials of new service features. If the user community appreciates the service, the company will enhance it in hopes of pulling in even more users to the service. If the feature is not well accepted, then the firm will drop it and shift the internal service enhancement efforts in another direction.

Speed of user growth and preparing next versions of their service offering to continue expansion are the focus of digital firm executives. Precise forecasts of competitive actions and external environment changes are secondary to the preparations necessary to ensure the firm can continue to grow and sustain the community of users. As the community grows, executives are preparing to approve the development of the next set of service enhancements to keep the service fresh and relevant to the community. Digital firm executives create scenarios of possibilities, although accuracy is less of a concern because the risk is not of error in a forecast but of being late to enhance a service offering, which would result in users abandoning the community.

NETWORK EFFECTS: AN OVERVIEW

"Network effects" is the economists' term to describe the interesting properties of the value of networks (or communities) to the participating members of the network. The value of networks to the members isn't always related to economic value, and the participants in networks are by no means limited to humans.

Consider the musk ox, the large, long-haired bovine that lives in the extreme north in a land without trees and covered in ice and snow for much of the year. Musk oxen have developed a rather unique network-oriented defense to protect themselves and their calves from their primary threat, which are wolves. When they perceive a threat, musk oxen instinctively form a circle with their rumps facing inward and their thick shaggy heads and horns facing outward ready to engage. The calves remain inside the circle with the bodies of the herd acting as a shield from the wolf pack. The wolves may attack the circle, but the oxen remain shoulder to shoulder to prevent the wolves from accessing the oxen's own vulnerable flanks and the calves. This defense has evolved and persisted because it works. It's also a helpful example of network effects.

If one single musk ox engaged wolves on the open tundra, it would be vulnerable to attack at its flank or rear, but if a second musk ox were present, the oxen could arrange themselves shoulder to shoulder, protecting one another's weak spots. The risk to the first ox drops significantly with the addition of the second ox. As more oxen join, the vulnerability drops even further. Consider a situation where seven oxen have arranged themselves in a circle, and an eighth ox standing off to the side witnesses the group fending off the wolves. This ox would surely see the immediate value of joining the group as quickly as possible in order to protect itself, not wanting to chance defending itself. Still, the value of the eighth ox joining the group is marginally less valuable to each of the existing group of seven because they have already achieved a great deal of security before its arrival.

The musk oxen's behavior demonstrates the basic principles of a network.

- Members of a network engaging in a valuable activity have interdependence created by interaction of each other's participation.
- During the early phases, when the network is relatively small, the network grows in value to each existing member with the addition of each new member, yet the potential attractiveness of joining the network is low when the network is small.
- As the network grows in membership, the increase in marginal value of each new member decreases to the existing members, while the attractiveness of joining the network increases.

We have used musk oxen behavior to describe network effects. Economists use the telephone network as their classic example. One person with a telephone and no one to call would be of relatively little value. A second person with a telephone increases the value of the device to the first person. The value of a telephone network with only two members may not be attractive to nonmembers, but as more people slowly acquire telephones, the network becomes more appealing. When a million people are in the network, it's much more attractive to nonmembers to join, but the additional marginal value of each new member to the existing members is small.

Waze is a firm that provides a digital service that advises users of the least congested traffic routes. Users are providing the company and its network with their current location, speed, and other similar data, which is aggregated with other Waze users to create a central mapping of congestion that can be used to smartly route users to their location, which saves each user time. Waze users also manually enter information about the route—whether there are, for example, stalled cars, police officers, or potholes. Obviously, the benefits of the network would be minuscule if there were only two drivers participating in the Waze community. But if every driver on the roads of a city were participating, the value of the service to each member would be significant.

With Waze, the benefit of being part of a user community represents value and in turn creates the incentives for users to be willing to share data about their own usage. The incentive to share usage data increases as more users join the community and use the service. A service that grows in value to users as participation increases has been termed by economists as demonstrating network effects. The more participants within the Waze community, the greater the value of the Waze service to each participant. Further, the more participants in the Waze community, the greater the incentive of those not participating to join and for current members to stay. This is often referred to as the network effect.

So in contrast to the economics of products that predict a decline in the value of the product with use over time, the value of a digital service that creates network effects increases with users and usage. This distinction creates some unique differences in the basis of competition between the world of information economics and the world of industrial economics. To be clear, not all digital services have the potential to create network effects across their user base, but those that can create an interdependency among users can benefit from dramatic growth in the user base and create a very powerful asset, which is an active user community.

THE CONVERGENCE OF CONNECTED ECONOMICS

The Connected World will bring the convergence of economic principles from both industrial *and* information economics *plus* the potential accelerator of network effects. Connected companies will create new business models that leverage the principles of this convergence. Executives within connected firms will become accustomed to the implications of having to both predict *and* prepare, as we show in figure 11. They'll have to be comfortable with the aspects of managing cost in a product world as well as understand offering zero-cost services to grow a user community as an asset for a future revenue stream in the digital world.

Firms coming from a product industry may decide to launch connected products at zero price and defer revenue until a large community of product users can be created. Firms coming from the internet or digital industry may decide to produce and launch connected products and use the products to give them access as a new entrant to a product industry. Each of these scenarios would have been highly improbable prior to connected economics.

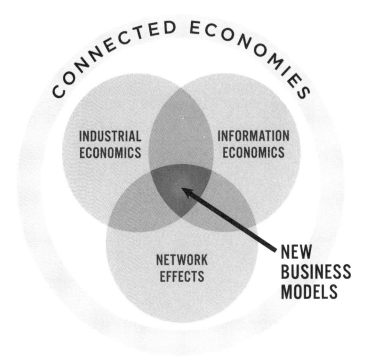

Figure 11 – The Emergence of Connected Economics.

We do understand that as product firms become connected firms, there will be, in the early phases of the
firm's transformation, a risk of executives assuming
that the principles they have learned from industrial
economics should be applied to the digital services
business. Some executives, for example, in launching
a connected product will expect that digital services
should be an incremental price for the product owner.
These executives have spent years practicing the idea
that when a new feature is added to a product the firm
generally offers it as an option, charging an incremental

price to cover the development cost and the variable costs of the feature.

Over time, these executives of former product firms will learn that charging fees to users to participate in the connected service user community will limit the participation of users and limit the availability of the product-in-use (PiU) data. Once the value of PiU data is fully recognized for its opportunity to understand the customer's usage of the product and the performance of the product, the executives will seek to eliminate any customer objection to participate. Executives in connected product firms will realize that when all product owners are members of the community that shares usage data, each and every product owner is now potentially more loyal to the product, and there is more usage data that can be used to develop additional revenue streams.

We have witnessed, over the past few years, the process of an industry progressively learning the value of the usage data from product owners as automotive original equipment manufacturers (OEMs) launched their initial connected product offerings. Initially, many auto OEMs launched these services as short-term free services. Upon expiration of the free period, customers would have to pay a subscription renewal fee to continue with the connected service. When product owners declined to renew the connected service, it was the OEMs that were worse off, not the customers. OEMs not only lost the revenue but also valuable key usage data about how the customers were using the car, how the car was performing, and the ability to create a market for additional connected services. They were losing the coveted PiU data. Over the last decade, more and more OEMs offering connected vehicle services have switched to making the core connected services standard "equipment" with the vehicle, removing any pricing obstacle to user participation and keeping the vehicle-in-use data flowing. OEMs are now collecting more data about both the vehicle performance and quality and the customer's lifestyle patterns. That data is now being used to lower vehicle warranty costs and enhance the opportunity to keep the customer's loyalty. This is an example of executives of a legacy product industry persisting in applying industrial economics to information economics services. This, the idea of "dominant logic," will be explored in chapter 3.

The risk of generalizing legacy economic principles also exists for digital service firms that consider producing a connected product to supplement its current digital service. We suspect that some prominent digital firms will explore the possibility of producing products to anchor their digital services and penetrate as a new entrant into an existing product industry. Google's parent company, Alphabet, the epitome of a digital service firm, has signaled that it may consider developing its own automobile customized to ergonomically complement its work related to autonomous driving services. Digital native firms may underestimate the complexity of building and scaling the production of physical products. Digital services firms may, based on their experience with the very low cost and rapid expansion of digital service communities, underappreciate the principles of industrial economics and the capital and operating costs associated with physical product. These high capital costs drive completely different income statements and balance sheets, and therefore encourage different investor profiles. There is likely to be a learning curve for top executives to understand the business of nonsoftware products as they continue this journey.

FORTUNE FAVORS THE PREPARED

In figure 11, we see that with Connected World economics, both legacy product and digital service executives will be able to expand the potential business models for their firms. Moving into the Connected World from either path, in other words, is possible. Both paths will be attempted. Some firms will succeed while others will fail. Success or failure, in some cases, will ultimately be reduced to whether the executives of the firms recognize the basic economic differences between being a legacy product or digital service firm and being a connected firm. More precisely, in some firms the time it will take to recognize the distinction between their dominant legacy business models and connected economics business models will determine whether they respond early or late relative to their competitors. Responding late will not be favorable for the firm.

The preceding sections highlight three very fundamental messages. The first is that the confluence of physical products with connected digital services will create connected economics that will become the crucible from which new connected business models will be forged. We show this in figure 12. Existing firms in product and digital industries will have a multitude of new ways to compete by adopting some, many, or all attributes of the other industry type. Barriers to entry in some industries will drop, allowing new entrants to move in. In other industries, the barriers to entry may actually be raised, locking out transitions into that industry to all firms except those with truly deep pockets looking to invest.

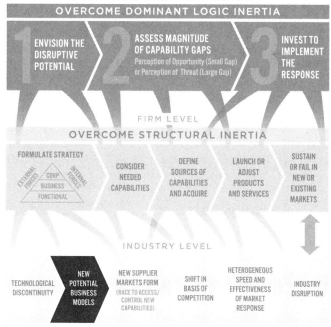

Figure 12 – CGS Advisors Core Transformation Framework—New Potential Business Models.

The second message is that the mash-up of industrial and information economics and network effects is creating a deep capability gap within the executives of firms coming from both internet and things industries as they contemplate the potential new business models. Legacy product executives have refined capabilities related to prediction and control. Digital or internet services executives are familiar with creating network effects on services that can be rapidly enhanced and deployed. They're unaccustomed to dealing with complex physical issues of forecasting demand for product and managing physical supply. The executive decision-making heuristics learned by partic-ipating in only one industry are likely to be insufficient to compete effectively in the Connected World.

Finally, as the chapter title suggests, we believe attempts to predict when the Connected World will reach their industry and what form it will take and which competitor will lead is a high-risk proposition. This is especially true when it comes to product firms. There is high certainty that the Connected World will disrupt the product indus-try. There is also high uncertainty about when it will start (it likely already has but not in public view). The message to firms resting in stable product-based industries is that they're at their most vulnerable at exactly this point in time. They must begin evaluating scenarios about existing competitors and new entrants launching new connected business models. Monitoring trends and accelerating the existing research and development road map isn't going to help. They must start to prepare for the new basis in competition and begin to act as if it's already too late.

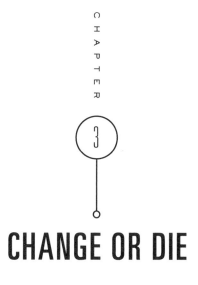

CHAPTER

3

CHANGE OR DIE

"Some will survive; most will not."

YOUR PAST CAN HOLD YOU IN PLACE

If you were to step back and reflect on the essence of the company for which you work, you'd marvel at the simplicity of its mission. It all started with the organization's founder, an entrepreneur, trying to take advantage of an opportunity in the marketplace. The mission was realized, and as the company prospered to an extent of sustainability, the *structure* in place became institutionalized. The structure we refer to is more than organizational structure but also inclusive of the processes, systems, and norms that allow workers to come in every day to work and repeat the same tasks in a rhythmic and consistent manner. Over successive business cycles, your company refined and optimized its capabilities to ensure the predictable and reliable delivery of whatever value it brought to the market. In the company's drive to achieve consistency, however, it has given up the option to be flexible and responsive to changes. Unfortunately, the stability of the company, which is an asset in predictable markets, can become a constraint as you try to adapt to compete in the connecting world.

The obligation of a leader at a product company no longer starts and ends with the engineering and production of the product. A service company leader can no longer see a discrete service that isn't intermingled with products and other services. As discussed in the last chapter, you'll have to utilize business models tuned to relevant economics in order to compete in this new landscape. You'll have to participate in the market for the data surrounding the product's consumption and its integration with other products and services. A business model that addresses data-driven digital services is significantly different than one that focuses solely on the manufacturing, delivery, and maintenance of products. In essence, you are potentially changing the organization for a dramatically new purpose that stands on the shoulders of the founder's original intent.

Meeting these challenges will necessitate that you and your leadership team refine your strategy to fit into this new connected marketplace. In order to successfully implement that strategy, you will need to transform the company's current capabilities to ones that support the purpose of the future company. The capabilities that your company currently has were created, refined, and hardened to serve that original founder's intent, which was likely formed before the world began connecting.

A natural consequence of hardening your business so it can consistently deliver a reliable product or service is likely that you and your leadership team have ended up seeing the world one way. You've likely learned so much about what success feels like in your current market that you may not have honed the skill to predict how the market will evolve. You probably don't even have the capabilities, at this stage, to see the magnitude of the transformation that your company will have to undergo in order to compete through the digital platforms that are increasingly driving the economy. Considering all this, change will likely prove difficult. Many will choose to sit back, observe, and consider their options. Don't!

SPEED MATTERS

So transforming your current company to compete in the Connected World will be a challenge given that the mix of capabilities that made it successful in the past aren't the same as those required for the future. The change is daunting, but maybe you imagine you can slowly and methodically make the shift. Markets, after all, don't shift overnight, so what is the big deal? Sorry, but it's imperative that your company moves quickly into the transformation process. Speed to market with new connected products and services operating in a new business model with new opportunities for differentiation will determine whether your company will be on the winning or losing side of the industry disruption. Firms that are fast to offer the initial connected products and services in their industries have opportunities to define the new markets; those that don't may miss the ability to truly influence the future landscape.

Early adopters of the technologies will establish customer expectations, because the companies that are first to market establish themselves as innovators in the minds of customers. These early entrants can set the price points for connected services and do it in their favor. They find the most critical integration points between connected experiences that cement them into the ecosystem. Speed to market with initial minimally viable products and services is an attribute of the economics of information, and it can lead to gains in market share at the expense of those firms that lag behind. It's precisely the differences in speed to market with new products and services that ultimately lead to the disruption of an existing industry. Fast responding firms of lower industry prominence can leap ahead of larger competitors that don't have a connected product or service offering.

Let's look at the other side of the speed to market issue. Firms slow to enter the market risk having to react to the offerings of the competitors, both new and established. They also risk losing existing customers who are curious about trying the new products or services being offered by competitors. Our research suggests that firms that are slow to introduce change into products and services typically begin a process of losing market share, and the declines have a high likelihood of becoming permanent. Companies once highly prominent within an industry that are unable to respond to changes in the basis of competition within their industry are the ones that are on the road to decline. Without a dramatic change in their responsiveness to the new market conditions, these laggards either end up as an acquisition for some of their redeeming capabilities or ultimately disband and cease to exist as a legal entity. In short, they die.

HOW TO BE FAST: STOP BEING SLOW!

So how do you avoid "death"? Clients and our MBA students occasionally ask versions of this question. How can firms rapidly transform into healthy Connected World participants? The key to speed is to stop being slow. Easy, right? Decades of studying and working on organizational transformation have shown us that many organizations are unable to internally transform because they're not aware of what's slowing them down. Quite simply, they have not thought about what it takes to be fast to react to a change in the external environment, change their internal capabilities, and get response into the market in the form of a new product or service.

We have studied and worked with firms that are fast and firms that are slow to respond to the same change in the external environment. Maybe it should seem that given an advancement in technologies from outside a certain industry, all things being equal, all the companies in an industry could respond to the change with a market response in about the same amount of time. In reality, things are not equal among firms, and time and time again, some firms will be fast in responding and others will be slow, and the bulk of the firms in an industry will be in the middle, a basic bell curve.

We have come to understand that there is a basic preliminary internal set of activities that each and every firm must complete when responding to a change in external environment. The speed with which a firm executes these activities determines the speed to market with a product or service change. We refer to these internal activities as the "First Mile" of response.

The one thing all fast organizations have in common is their ability to quickly execute, or even sprint, that first mile. The executives of these fast-moving companies either have a defined process in place to take them through those early steps, or they operate with intuition and awareness regarding the external environment, the current industry basis of competition, and the organization's internal capabilities. Comparatively, the executives of slower-responding firms maybe get mired in defining an internal process that has sufficient participation of the entire executive structure. They refuse to execute the First Mile unless there is total consensus, which only comes with excessive deliberations and the wasting of time. They plod through the First Mile and consequently show up late or not at all in the marketplace.

RUNNING THE FIRST MILE

Competing in the connecting world is a journey that has no discernable end point. The horizon is crowded with emerging technologies readying for convergence. Although the end isn't clear, the starting point should be—it has already passed. It's imperative companies get into the race and see it as a race. We can break down the First Mile into three distinct steps.

Step one of the First Mile—Envision the Disruptive Potential—calls on leaders to gain perspective and accurately consider the implications of the technological change on the current state of competition within their current industry and within emerging industries. Executives must determine if the change will have zero, some, or major impact. Envisioning a future shift in the competitive landscape requires considerable foresight. We can even count it as an internal executive team capability. It means you must question if the connected technologies could change future industry business models, the industry's current relationship with customers, or change the barriers to entering the industry. If the answer to any or all of these questions is yes, then it would appear that this technology does have the potential to disrupt the current industry. It could even mean that it could reshape the boundaries of the industry itself. What this truly means is that there could be winners and losers defined based on how fast and how well the companies respond to the technological discontinuity. If you have been reading up until this point, you know we think that the answer is clearly yes for all industries.

Failing to recognize or significantly underestimating the industry disruptive potential of the connected technologies means not believing in the industry disruptive potential. This could be a conclusion that the impact on the existing industry will not be dramatic, or that it will be more or less easily absorbed by firms uniformly across the industry. The implication of this conclusion is that nothing further will happen inside the organization. Until executives understand and then believe in the disruptive potential, there will be no meaningful response from the firm, period. (Read more about this step in chapters 4 and 5.)

In the second step of the First Mile—Assess Magnitude of Capability Gaps—the company's executives must assess the degree to which the organization has access to the capabilities necessary to "connect" their company. To execute this assessment, executives must have an objective and clear understanding of both the firm's current capabilities and those needed to compete in the connecting world. In most cases, it will not simply be a matter of adding new capabilities. It's likely to mean that within the current portfolio of capabilities, some existing capabilities will require enhancement while others will prove constraining and need to be dampened or eliminated. The difference in magnitude between the portfolio of current capabilities and those necessary to launch a connected product or service is the capability gap. The larger the capability gap, the larger the company transformation necessary in order to get a product into the marketplace. The size of the capability gap certainly can impact the speed of getting a connected product or service initially into the marketplace. Companies that have a small gap will generally be faster. Firms with large capability gaps are able to overcome the gap through acquisition or aggressive use of third-party services and suppliers.

What is certain is that failing to identify the necessary capabilities to create connected products or services will result in an inability to formulate and implement a response. Executives of companies that are slow to understand what it will actually take in terms of capabilities are typically slow to launch a market response. Companies that underestimate the magnitude of the gap and launch a transformation effort that is underscoped will also be slow to market, given that their transformations will likely be plagued with starts and stops as they struggle to define all that they need to do. (We explore this in greater detail in chapter 6.)

In the third and final phase of the First Mile—Invest to Implement the Response—executives must determine if the company has the necessary internal resources—skilled people and money—to acquire the necessary capabilities and implement a market response. To fund the transformation process means redeploying existing resources away from some other use. The availability of slack resources, such as cash on hand, outside those necessary to operate the current business, will be a consideration for all companies. Some firms will have the "deep pockets" of slack resources available to acquire the capabilities. This will help a company be faster to acquire the capabilities and put them to work to deliver the response. Companies with fewer slack resources are faced with a dilemma of whether they should redeploy existing resources from current operations to fund the transformation. Finding the balance between managing the present and building for the future when resources are scarce is likely to be a deliberate process and runs the risk of slowing down the transition. The inability or the reluctance of executives to commit the necessary investments will, of course, slow or even stop the firm from responding to the Connected World. Lacking the commitment to spend, or having only a partial commitment, will result in, at best, a delayed or, at worst, no response in the market. Being brave in these times of transformation isn't easy, but it is necessary. (We touch on this in chapter 7.)

OPPORTUNITY OR THREAT DEFINES THE PACE

The First Mile description is the culmination of many years' worth of research and experience, and it boils down to the following simple sequence of logic. Executives who see the magnitude of the pending industry change, who understand what capabilities are necessary to respond, are willing and able to invest to acquire the capabilities, and then aggressively use them to make it happen, will be fast to market.

Of the three steps, it's the first that is shared among the leaders of first responding firms. They envision the disruptive potential of the change. It will be the same for the emergence of the Connected World. Those firms whose executives see the direction their industry is moving toward will ultimately be the most motivated to take action.

Still, there are some additional patterns in the speed at which firms adapt to change. Assume top executives of two different firms each believe that the Connected World has large disruptive potential. In the second step, where they are to assess the capability gap, one firm has identified that it has a relatively small internal capability gap while the other firm has a much larger gap. The executives of the firm with the small gap are more likely to see the connected technologies as an "opportunity" to be exploited and will, therefore, be the fastest to commit the necessary investments and introduce a connected product or service. New entrants to an industry may be among the first to respond with new products and services, especially if they're entering from another industry where connected capabilities were more the norm.

Conversely, executives of firms with a large capability gap are more likely to see the connecting world as a threat, given that they must undertake a significant transformation effort to be prepared for competition in the Connected World. Whether the threatened executives lead their firms to a fast market response will depend on additional factors. Executives with deep pockets who feel a potential loss of prominence within the industry will be more willing and able to make the investment to close the capability gap and will also be faster to make the commitment and get products and services to market.

Firms with leaders who see the disruptive potential of the Connected World with the smallest capability gap will be the bravest. Looking to score first, they'll become first movers and likely introduce connected products and services to an industry. The second fastest firms will be those that see the disruptive potential and actually have a large capability gap and have the deep pockets to invest in acquiring an entire existing third-party firm or to create an entirely new division or business unit to grow the capabilities. These leaders are motivated more from a position of fear, which is an equally powerful emotion.

What about leaders and firms that don't immediately see the opportunity or the risk? What if you allow your firm to be slow?

INERTIA IN ORGANIZATIONS

Organizational inertia has been defined as the "delay or failure" of an organization to effectively adapt to events that occur in the external environment. The easiest way to measure the effects of inertia is to consider the delay between the first firm to introduce meaningful connected products or services and the other companies in the industry. Firms slow to market are demonstrating the symptoms of inertia. They appear to be unchanging, although the delay in and of itself isn't the problem. The delay, in fact, is inevitable. That these delays aren't equally distributable across the industry is what leads to difficulties for companies. The heterogeneity in response to changes in the environment is what will lead to industry disruption and create winners and losers.

Two different sources of inertia within organizations impact the completion of the First Mile. One source is within the heads of individuals, while the second is embedded within the structure of the organization itself.

- Dominant Logic Inertia: This falls squarely at the feet, or rather in the hearts and minds, of the firm's leaders and their ability to recognize and choose to react.
- Structural Inertia: This is the relative slowness caused by the firm's systems, people, and culture, which are aligned to today's strategy and aren't able to support the new, or in this case, the "connected strategy."

These two sources of inertia are prominent in the transformation framework and highlighted in figure 13. Each is displayed across its full journey, because the effects can attack every part of the First Mile.

Overcoming dominant logic inertia is the responsibility of

executives. You'll need to reflect on your own judgment system as you consider a response to the connecting world. The second source sits between the executives and the firm layers. The source of structural inertia is the structure itself. It's tied deeply into the fabric that makes up the firm. Battling the inertia will need to be a significant part of the transformation.

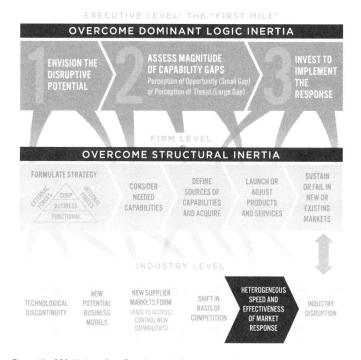

Figure 13 – CGS Advisors Core Transformation Framework – Sources of Inertia.

THE DOGMA OF THE DOMINANT LOGIC

Dominant logic inertia is the leader's bias. It's the sum of all the leader's mental models about his or her company and the industry in which it competes. This bias is accumulated through years of experience where the leader observes, feels, and determines the "way things work." It defines an understanding of best practices and tactics to be used by the company in the industry. It's also the awareness of inevitable market cycles and the ability to accurately predict outcomes before they happen. These are best practices programmed in the minds of the leaders who have steered them to the top of the organization and industry. The dominant logic is a source of delay in responding to an external change, especially when people and, more importantly, leaders of companies don't perceive that the change will impact their industry or company. The dominant logic is exposed when an executive says, "I know this industry, and the Connected World doesn't apply here."

DON'T END UP LIKE A BOILED FROG

You've likely heard the story of the boiled frog. A frog finds itself in a pot of tepid water. The water is slowly brought to a boil. Because the change in temperature is gradual, the frog is comfortable in the pot and unaware that it's boiling to death. The frog perceives no risk and is unable to add up the incremental environmental changes and reflect on what it means for the not-so-distant future. If anything, the warming water feels comforting. Eventually, by the time the frog does realize what's happening, it has lost any ability to jump out of the pot. Its comfort with the water combined with its inattentiveness to accumulating small changes made it "blind" to the risk that was encroaching.

The above parable is the essence of the impact of industry dominant logic on leaders inside stable industries. Over the years, they have grown comfortable with their mental models about industry norms and confident in their ability to direct their companies. The environment, however, is slowly changing around industries and organizations. The connecting world is slowly emerging across many industries, and the pace of change is accelerating. Some firms are leading with innovative new products and services. There's no way you and your fellow business leaders aren't aware of the revolutionary business models changing whole industries. News stories about the Internet of Things (IoT), sensors connecting products to humans and other products, and services such as Airbnb and Uber are widespread. As a consumer, you most probably enjoy taking advantage of these digital platforms. Meanwhile, you're underestimating their impact if you think of these services as nothing more than "neat features, entertainment, or nice-to-have curiosities." These changes are encroaching on your industry as well. Don't be like the frog that fails to internalize what is happening in its surrounding environment and what it means for its survival.

The dominant logic prevents executives of companies from being able to envision the real disruptive potential of the connecting world on their industry. Changes to patterns do occur over time, but these changes have been evolutionary and are recognized post hoc as reinforcing the long wave patterns. Executives use their experiences to create rules about how to respond to the pattern. The longtime executive is often heard saying, "I've seen this all before, and this is just another cycle." The longer a person has experienced limited change, the less likely they are to see major change coming. They are, in essence, blind to potentials outside the horizon of their experiences, and they cannot be expected to travel the First Mile until the potential is revealed to them.

Some leaders can see other pots beginning to boil near them, but they cannot sense the temperature of their own environment increasing. They may think the water will get warmer, but not for some time. Consequently, they don't complete step one of the First Mile, and their firms remain inert. There is no externally observable response from their firm to the connecting technologies.

Blindness to the disruptive potential of the IoT and the Connected World is a major source of inertia and a major contributor to companies reacting late to the technological discontinuity. Blaming them for this failure to notice may be unfair. After all, this disruption isn't something they've seen before, and they may not even fully understand it. They may not even be able to tell if it's real. Still, at the end of the day, leaders are responsible for their own paralysis. The choice to allow inertia to take over is a choice to not deal with the future.

We expect industry dominant logic will continue surfacing in executive suites as people begin to contemplate the implications of the Connected World. Some firms have recognized the risks of falling under the dogma of dominant industry logic and have begun filling executive vacancies with candidates from outside their current industry, specifically for the purpose of introducing diversity of thought about patterns. You may want to start having an outward-in look for your own area of responsibility.

WILLFULLY BLIND?

A second form of executive blindness to the disruptive potential to change in the external environment is what we would call willful blindness. Top executives are smart people. They've arrived at their current positions because they've demonstrated an ability throughout their careers to connect the dots. They can grasp how once a sensor is embedded in a diaper and becomes a key diagnostic device in the health of infants, the company selling the diaper is transformed into a product and services company. Also, they read newspapers and industry and business publications. They're aware of how disruptors such as Facebook, Airbnb, Uber, Samsung's SmartThings, and Amazon have upended entire industries.

The willful part of the blindness comes because in their current jobs they're rewarded for stability, predictability, and short-term results. It's obvious that the future is going to be different, and the company will have to respond. Nevertheless, they undergo an internal calculation that confirms it's not worth jeopardizing the current rewards for the sake of taking the company on a risky journey with an unknown outcome. Perhaps the leader's compensation package is tied to quarterly stock performance. Suggesting the creation of an entirely new division to explore ways in which the company can profit off product end-use data will not enhance the stock price in the short term. These are the calculations that surely occur in the top echelons of companies. Retirement is probably near for most of those leaders, and it's easy for them to rationalize that shifting the business model to meet future challenges is a task better left to the next generation of leaders.

Executives at the top may see an escape route from the boiling pot, because in many cases they'll be out of the game before the new hierarchy takes form. However, you don't have that luxury if you are a leader in the level below, or the "junior executive." This may be your opportunity to position yourself as a change agent within the organization, the person who is constantly measuring the water's temperature and taking the time and effort to point out repeatedly that competing in the connecting world is going to be something different. It may be your opportunity to be deputized today and become tomorrow's connected leader.

DOING THE DANCE YOU KNOW

The concept of preservation of self is another reason executives may adopt a position of willful blindness. The leaders see the coming change, and even are aware of the necessity for the company to respond, but they recognize that competing in the Connected World is entering an unfamiliar world. Executives may fear that they don't have the capabilities to lead in this different industry context, especially because they cannot say with complete confidence where the company is headed.

Most leaders will stick with what they know works even after they recognize it may no longer fit the environment. They don't change their approaches because they're not familiar or confident with any other way. It's not much different than what happens when you find yourself on the dance floor. The music starts playing and you do the dance you know. Usually, you can trace your style back to a specific time in your life, probably a joyful, significant moment, such as sharing a dance with a parent, or a first love. It's a moment on the dance floor when you felt comfortable with your body and self, and your movements felt natural. From that moment forward, you find yourself repeating the same moves every time you hit the dance floor. No matter what the tune, the beat, or the style of music, you have your comfort moves. The positive feedback you've received from your partner and the other dancers over the years has encouraged you to continue using those same moves. When you try some other flashy moves you've caught on television, you feel clumsy.

The leaders at the top of an organization will dance the same dance that got them promoted from junior positions to the upper levels of the company. They'll see the promotions and rewards received along the way as clear proof that the other executives, the board, and shareholders approve of the way they move. Also, they can feel how they're in sync with the members of the organization, which has brought the company success in everything they do, from how they deal with customers, to how ideas pass through the organization. Success will continue, they believe, as long as they continue making the same moves in an unchanging environment.

What if suddenly the music begins to change? The beat speeds up. It's clear you'll have to adjust your style, because you find yourself tripping over your own feet. It has been a long while since you learned a dance move, and you continue to try what you know. It has always paid off. There's no reason in your mind why you and the other leaders in the company can't continue to be rewarded for the same type of decisions the company has been making in the boardroom for the past several decades. Even if you see that the rules of the game have started to shift because the value systems of buyers and customers are changing, it will still take a compelling reason to move you away from this reflexive, or familiar, behavior. You won't look awkward on the dance floor if all of the other leaders are tripping over their own feet as well. You must, however, carefully listen to the music. Find the parts of the song built from the music you know, and identify which new styles have been added. Learning new dance moves isn't impossible; it can even be fun. It does, however, take a wider perspective and openness to the new music being played.

STRUCTURAL INERTIA CAN FOIL THE PLAN

Even if leaders are able to get over the dominant logic dilemma, they're not out of the woods yet. They still need to shift the structure of the organization to change the portfolio of capabilities necessary for the connecting world. It starts with step two of the First Mile—Defining the Capability Gap. Having a great product or service is necessary but no longer sufficient for having a competitive advantage in the connecting world. Competing in this new landscape requires capabilities that, most probably, don't exist inside the organization and potentially not even within the current industry. Supplementing the current capabilities portfolio of the company with new capabilities is a tall order for the executives of an organization managing success with unconnected products, or services that aren't informed by information flowing from products in use.

Understanding the structural composition of the current portfolio of internal capabilities isn't a trivial task, because capabilities are the result of a complex layering and integration of internal structural elements within the organization. Structure doesn't refer only to the organizational structure held by an HR department. It has a broader definition and includes all elements created to deliver on the founder's intent. It includes the information technology systems, the processes, the information, goals, human motivations, as well as the culture. It's everything that makes the company operationally repeatable from day to day. Describing what new structure must be created to support those new capabilities is even more complex but is necessary to define the capability gap.

Executives in firms that can't adequately describe the details of the new capabilities will be reluctant to move forward into the connecting world. The result is a delayed or unobservable response in the market. The firm, continuing with the current capability profile, will appear inert. Eventually, it may determine to add, change, or delete capabilities, but it will reach this second milestone later than other firms in the industry.

If you've ever had to change one IT system inside your organization, you'll immediately appreciate the difficulty of any systemic change, which is what will need to happen if you plan on defending your spot in the value chain of the Connected World. Even changing a fairly simple IT system that supports the accounting function can cost hundreds of thousands of dollars and take many months to complete, if not longer. Consider the potential changes needed to support the business models of the Connected World. If a simple back office function takes significant budget and time, what will the transformation of the whole business feel like? It can be overwhelming. The complexity of defining the capability gap in terms of the necessary structural changes and the time associated with all of that effort is structural inertia.

Structural lock-in is natural and is hugely positive in times of stability. It allows for the recognition of efficiencies and stable market positions. Unfortunately, we are not in stable times. Even if the income statement appears stable today, the marketplace is shifting. Understand your structure to a degree that you can efficiently change it, so it does not prevent you from shifting your strategy.

Structure supports today's strategy, yet it can constrain tomorrow's.

Unfortunately, there will likely be some peripheral and compounding structural challenges that exist outside of your company and that you have limited ability to influence. A company, to a large degree, is deeply tied to the actions and organizational health of its suppliers (upstream) and distribution partners (downstream). Just as your company may experience inertia from the effort to adjust capabilities, so will the companies your organization relies on. If you're changing the way you do business, you'll need these value chain partners to keep pace with you. These companies in the supply chain are dealing with their own internal structure and strategic choice issues. They may even be providing the same function to your other competitors in the same industry. If you were to ask them to put a sensor in a component when none of their other customers are making similar requests, they may refuse, explaining that their business isn't built to deliver embedded sensors.

DOWNSTREAM INERTIA

Finally, there are risks of inertial effects in step three of the First Mile—Invest to Implement the Response. Assuming a company has successfully envisioned the disruptive potential of the Connected World and has adequately measured the magnitude of the capability gap, the next step is where the "rubber hits the road." The company must now commit resources and change the direction of the company. Steps one and two of the First Mile are essential, but they are mere preparation for step three, where the investment stage of the journey occurs. Without investing to close the capability gap, and without then using those adapted capabilities to launch a new connected product or service, there is no market response. The firm, despite its internal thinking, is still more or less inert and stuck in its past.

Inertia in step three can be the result of a number of issues. The first and most obvious is that the firm just doesn't have the slack resources to close the capability gap, either because the gap is so great, or because the firm is lean and struggling to survive in today's environment. This dilemma is truly a challenge. Firms barely surviving in stable industries are unlikely to make the transition to compete in a changed industry context. The switching costs exceed the firm's ability to pay. The hope for survival for these companies is largely based on being acquired and potentially absorbed into a firm that has a greater likelihood to close the capability gap.

The dominant logic also rears its head again in this third phase. Some top executives, while skeptical about the true disruptive potential of the connecting world, have at least permitted an internal review of the capability gap so they can better understand the magnitude of the investment necessary to compete. This is likely to be a common occurrence inside the executive suite of companies, and it's a pragmatic approach in that it creates the option of executing step three without committing. It's a form of preparation in the absence of prediction. During the time of executing steps one and two, the executives can be monitoring other firms in their industry to determine if they seem to be poised to launch their own market response. Holding short of investing in new capabilities and developing a competitive response is not a strategy that will result in any first mover advantage. Rather, it may fit with a company whose executives have decided that being a fast follower into the Connected World is a more comfortable approach. The dominant logic influence slows the responsiveness of the company but does not prevent a response altogether. Firms that have a large capability gap to close and possess a limited amount of slack resources to invest into a changing industry—they can't afford to be wrong—may decide there's too much risk in trying to hit a moving target.

Most leaders we poll think that the smallest, most agile companies are the ones best poised to shift into the Connected World. They're only partially correct. Small firms lack the complexity of change, so they typically do not suffer from structural inertia in phase three. They can pivot into the connecting world as long as leaders drive them there. Surprisingly, large firms, the most prominent ones in an unconnected industry, may also have an advantage that will lead to survival, such as high levels of available slack resources. These market-leading firms typically will have complex internal structures, high employee counts, and high-volume supplier contracts, which will tend to make them slower to close the capability gap. They are like an ocean freighter trying to turn. Some large firms manage quick initial transitions toward a market response despite their size. These firms are likely to view the disruptive potential of the connecting world as a threat to their current prominence. They are the market leaders whose market share is the target of the smaller and newer firms that may see early adoption of connected capabilities as a means to steal share. These large firms have in the past adopted a couple of different approaches to leveraging their deep pockets to invest in closing the capability gap and developing a market offering.

One tactic has been to acquire an existing firm in another industry that has the capabilities. In chapter 5, we will discuss the phenomenon of automotive OEMs buying ride sharing companies to add those capabilities to the OEMs' profile if they deem them necessary for a connected mobility service. Acquisitions involve complexities related to integration of services with the acquiring company. This can slow efficiency of the acquisition, but it does immediately bring new capabilities under the firm's control. A second tactic some larger firms have used is to create their own separate subsidiary as a start-up with the mandate to build the necessary capabilities. The parent firm provides the investment necessary to support the growth of the company. Although the start-up is beginning from scratch, it does have the advantage of not having to continuously compete with the parent company for resources and shared services. The negotiation of internal transfer costs, prices, and service levels to create the capabilities inside the parent company's structure can stall and eventually stop progress on building new capabilities from inside a company. Some large companies, therefore, have decided that it is faster to create new capabilities in a new, autonomous, well-funded start-up subsidiary. This was the approach General Motors executives took with the creation of OnStar decades ago. OnStar services may have never made it to the market if it had been developed within the automotive company and competing with the multiple brands for resources and attention to development priorities.

If you are a midsized company leader, you should carefully consider this journey. You have enough structure to make step three of the First Mile difficult, and your pockets may not be as deep as some of the larger market leaders. Speed may be the most important element for you, so stare down the sources of inertia, eradicate them where you can, and get on your way.

THE COST OF INERTIA

Once upon a time, the consumer mobile communications industry was all about hardware. A company such as Nokia dominated because consumers wanted the devices they produced. Over time, users began to place greater value on the phones' operating systems, apps ecosystem, and content. Nokia failed to adapt to this change and was pushed out of the market, eventually selling to another industry player. This was a company that had already pivoted successfully years before in moving from the paper production industry to one that sold electronic hardware. Yet, its inability to pull off a double pivot doomed it. In 2007, it held fifty percent of the global mobile phone market share. By 2013, that number was down to the low single digits.

On its face, there may not be a better example of a company and its leadership that effectively and profitably transitioned, especially when we consider that there is no obvious relationship between paper and electronic hardware. The reality, though, is that the second pivot was much more significant. Nokia was a hardened product company when it was selling paper. When it transformed into an electronic hardware company, it was still selling products. The second pivot away from a product company into a services company, one that ran on software platforms, proved to be too drastic and difficult to execute.

In a best-case scenario, a failure to adapt will end with

your company becoming a supplier for another company. RIM (the maker of the BlackBerry brand), another once-market-leader in the mobile phone industry, held close to 20 percent of the global market share at its peak. Users loved their devices for their easy-to-use keyboards and email experience. Enterprises loved their security and ease of integration. It, too, rode the benefits of being a solid hardware producer with capabilities that fit enterprise decision makers. Meanwhile, it never could make the leap to consumer-driven digital platforms. Although most end users believe BlackBerry is a relic from the pre-smartphone era, the reality is far more complex. Its security capabilities proved valuable, and they, through licensing agreements, have found their way into the devices of other companies. In essence, it has become component suppliers to the major players in the Connected World ecosystem. Still, RIM's prominence in the industry has dropped dramatically. Instead of being an industry leader, it has become a case study of what happens when a business fails to respond to changes.

Now is the time for you to decide how you want your company to participate in the Connected World. Opting to try and keep your position in the industry would require reshaping your company so it can deliver a product experience that relies on added layers of service. It may be you conclude that your best option is to continue doing what you do best, even if it means a loss of prominence. This doesn't mean you can continue operating as if nothing has changed. In this scenario, you'll need to form the right partnerships with the firms that will matter in this new landscape. The third option is to avoid making a decision. Know that if you choose this option, the other companies, consumers, and supply chains will ultimately make the decision for you.

Industry disruption is a significant change in relative prominence of individual firms in the industry. Firms that fail to adapt in a timely or meaningful manner to the technological discontinuity risk a decline in prominence, which can be measured in revenue and market share. The greatest consequence, however, is losing the ability to determine your organization's fate in the emerging ecosystem. Your company will lose its autonomy to create its own corporate strategy. It will lose the ability to define what business it's in. Whereas your company used to define the industry, the industry will now define the company based on the value and capabilities it retains. The industry may even decide that your company lacks commercial viability, in which case, the end result is insolvency, bankruptcy, and "death."

Leaders value the right to chart their own course for their firm, as they should. Workers take pride in the role the company they work for plays in an industry. Many people prefer to work for final good manufacturers with recognized brands, as opposed to component suppliers, because they want a company that isn't dependent on the success, decisions, and whims of other companies. Suppose you're an executive at an automotive OEM that fails to adapt to the Connected World. Overnight, your business becomes a component supplier for another company's autonomous vehicle service. Your brand will still exist, but it will be part of a fleet, potentially buried behind a digital experience a service operator controls. That will be a bitter pill for you the leader and your workers to swallow, and it's a change that will go right to your personal and professional identity.

It's a real possibility that your firm will go from being a prominent apex predator to a grazer, the target of acquisition. What will it mean for you as a leader to be associated with a brand and company that failed to make the transition because you were unable to recognize the disruptive potential of the new technologies? Many of the willfully blind executives of your organization will not suffer the fallout. They will have left with their golden parachutes. Dealing with the aftereffects will fall on you. It's hard on the head and ego to know that you had a role in a company that has flamed out. Ultimately, if the company is inert, it's because you, as a leader, were inert. It's not difficult to see the changes already under way in your industry. This is about your career moving forward and the choice of whether you'll turn a blind eye or accept the challenge to locate the critical map to produce an observable external response for your company. Embrace change, or be part of the death march.

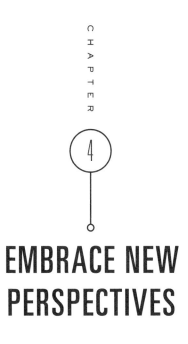

EMBRACE NEW PERSPECTIVES

"Envision the disruptive potential."

When deciding how you'll navigate your firm to adapt to the connecting world, you first must change the way you look at the business environment. Most transitioning companies struggle to see past the space where their products or services currently operate. They function within the constraints and possibilities of their own industry, constantly looking over their shoulders at the known competition. Yesterday's product, and everything they know about it and the industry, ends up informing the product and service they are creating for tomorrow. This results in missing crucial elements about the emerging landscape. For example, they may not even see that they'll be moving into an adjacent or even a completely different industry.

They may ultimately decide that they aren't prepared to move into this highly digital world where they're expected to produce the traditional product along with the data-oriented services it provides. Perhaps manufacturing and design are what they do well, and it's what they want to continue doing. If they choose, however, to continue having a relationship with their traditional customer base, because that's their strength, they'll need to think beyond the edges of their traditional industry space. This doesn't mean looking at industries that are similar to their own for inspiration. In fact, the familiar can act as a constraint. Instead, they will need to examine the context in which their customers are using their products and services and look to best combine the experiences from adjacent companies and industries.

Let's take the case of a car company that's made the decision to take those initial steps toward transformation. The company, looking at other industries associated with its own, assumes the new model is about getting people from point A to point B. It refashions itself as a mobility company. Not only may it decide to start producing additional vehicles such as trucks, buses, and special purpose vehicles, but it also resolves to provide the function of helping these vehicles operate, whether through automation or some type of human-based service. Meanwhile, their primary competitors, in trying to see the future, are looking far beyond the industries typically associated with passenger cars. When they look at these adjacent industries, it's clear that the new model isn't only about moving people. Rather, it's about the information gleaned from the vehicles and services used for transportation. They refashion themselves as data-oriented companies interested in making the movement of people and goods more efficient. It's about fitting this movement into other value chains and ultimately about making people's lives easier. These competitors may succeed, because they've managed to break from their familiar world and witness trends and apply technologies from dissimilar industries to push to support across industry. These connected experiences are the fabric of the Connected World.

It is the executive leader's role to envision what the future looks like in the Connected World, how customers, businesses, or consumers will experience their product and services in the future. This perspective requires executives to look to both the firm and industry(ies) levels to gain the proper perspective, as seen in figure 14.

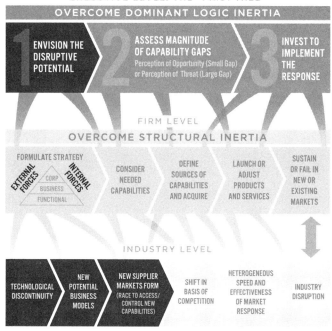

OVERCOME DOMINANT LOGIC INERTIA

1 ENVISION THE DISRUPTIVE POTENTIAL

2 ASSESS MAGNITUDE OF CAPABILITY GAPS
Perception of Opportunity (Small Gap) or Perception of Threat (Large Gap)

3 INVEST TO IMPLEMENT THE RESPONSE

FIRM LEVEL

OVERCOME STRUCTURAL INERTIA

FORMULATE STRATEGY
EXTERNAL FORCES / INTERNAL FORCES
CORP
BUSINESS
FUNCTIONAL

CONSIDER NEEDED CAPABILITIES

DEFINE SOURCES OF CAPABILITIES AND ACQUIRE

LAUNCH OR ADJUST PRODUCTS AND SERVICES

SUSTAIN OR FAIL IN NEW OR EXISTING MARKETS

INDUSTRY LEVEL

TECHNOLOGICAL DISCONTINUITY

NEW POTENTIAL BUSINESS MODELS

NEW SUPPLIER MARKETS FORM (RACE TO ACCESS/ CONTROL NEW CAPABILITIES)

SHIFT IN BASIS OF COMPETITION

HETEROGENEOUS SPEED AND EFFECTIVENESS OF MARKET RESPONSE

INDUSTRY DISRUPTION

Figure 14 – CGS Advisors Core Transformation Framework – Envision the Disruptive Potential.

PUT THE PERSON IN THE MIDDLE

There was a time when product companies thinking about the connected future would put their product in the middle with the customer as one more thing the product would touch in its life cycle. Preparing for the Connected World starts with seeing the end consumer in the middle, with your product and service as just one of a large connected web of other products and services making up a user experience. This moves your company away from the traditional model of marketing the built product to the consumer. Instead, you must understand the consumer's usage of the product and see what's happening in and around this space on a transactional basis. From this information, you can begin thinking about how your product or service fits in with the other services in the consumer's life. This will provide a fuller picture of the entire network, or the customer-centric ecosystem. We often use figure 15 to help leaders imagine the world that surrounds their end user, and how they need to consider designing their business to support the full experience.

Figure 15 – Ecosystem View for Designers of the Connected World.

In the Connected World, potentially more than fifty percent of a product's or service's value will come from how seamlessly it fits into the user's ecosystem. It's about the effectiveness of connections and allowing entities to collaborate and create a unified experience for the user. These customers will judge the product or service on how seamlessly they work with other products and services in order to form a complete experience. Imagine a world where users may never have to take the step of integrating one product with another one. The product or service automatically informs the other products and services in the ecosystem. People will come to expect that nothing will have to be done on their end to reorient the product to make it compatible with whatever else the person is using.

The above description is the difference between having to type the address into a car's navigation system and the transportation service vehicle knowing the address ahead of time because it read the passenger's calendar. The seamlessness of the integration doesn't stop here. The vehicle or mobility service will also anticipate traffic conditions, the price of transportation, and the preferences of not only the driver but also all the other travelers. All of this is a precursor to a vehicle that navigates itself, without ever showing the route to the driver. The trust between the vehicle and the driver has already been brokered, and the person knows the vehicle has his or her best interests in "mind" when it comes to variables such as route and price.

The competitors in the marketplace that manage to design and engineer their products to fit into the ecosystem, which stretches far beyond a singular industry, are the ones who will succeed. Those who leave it to the consumer to manage how it integrates into the ecosystem may end up surviving but will be competing with an isolated product and, possibly, a novelty item. They'll draw from a small pool of nostalgic customers. In a world of autonomous cars, there will still be people who will want to drive the car and not be relegated to being a passenger in the back seat. Over time, however, this pool of individuals will shrink. After all, people still ride horses but only for sport. Catering to a niche market is a different business, one without much room for competition.

In this new world, it's not going to be enough to build a refrigerator that's simply an appliance in the kitchen. Customers will expect that the information from their lives will inform their use of the product. An appliance such as the refrigerator will be seen as the last point on the food value chain, perhaps playing the role of automatically replenishing food from the most efficient or cheapest food service in the region, depending on the preferences of the user. Because it's the last station before the food enters the body, it will play a part in the user's connection to the health and wellness industries, similar to the scenario that was shared in the introduction to this book. It won't be enough to create a sleek-looking appliance with a smaller access door and mood lighting.

Consumers and competitors will view your product as half as valuable as an equivalent product that's connected and integrated with a full-connected service experience. If you aren't connected, you'll be competing with half the value of your competitors. Allowing your competitors to take the lead, waiting to see how the network they create looks, isn't a winning strategy. Low barriers to entry do allow companies to rush into the connecting world, but the barriers are raised as industries and companies begin to connect. The ability for individual competitors to differentiate themselves on product alone diminishes as the value of the connections goes up. It's the ones who connect first that will embed themselves in this seamless flow of information. The longer you wait, in other words, the more your competitors are locking themselves into this new ecosystem, which means you're locking yourself out. A lagging firm may be able to enter a small fragment of the connected ecosystem, but once the primary players emerge and the industries begin to stabilize, it will become difficult to gain access to the information network, a crucial component of connected services. Those companies within the ecosystem are operating in a new form of competition and collaboration. Data from multiple sources is a currency that connects people's lives together. This will create open and closed ecosystems. For companies embedded within an ecosystem, granting access to new companies to join requires some degree of mutual consent. Access may not be forthcoming for companies that attempt to participate later.

Once you identify your organization's place in the ecosystem, you'll look at value differently. You'll have to consider whether you're producing a product customers will purchase, or if it works better as a service. For example, in the jet engine industry there came a point when the manufacturers changed their business models. The transition to a service was enabled through the product's in-use data gathered over some years that allowed the manufacturers to see in real time how the engine was performing and become highly proficient in understanding how to diagnose problems before they occur. It allowed the OEM to understand the product in an entirely different way. Instead of selling the engines to the airline manufacturer, they adopted a model of selling flight power to the airlines, guaranteeing a certain amount of uptime. They knew their product so well that they no longer had to sell a product. They could give customers what they wanted. As the American economist Theodore Levitt said, "People don't want to buy a quarter-inch drill; they want a quarter-inch hole." Unfortunately, when a customer goes to the hardware store, he or she doesn't have the option to buy the hole, so the person is forced to buy the tool, even if it's the only hole they need to make. One of the more significant changes in the Connected World is the sudden ability to buy the most relevant experience instead of the product.

A warning, however. Even the tendency to follow your customer's lead is another potential constraint for companies trying to develop a new way of looking at the world. Basing innovation solely on current customer feedback is problematic because your current customers aren't the ones who can fuel a paradigm shift. They are only your most recent customers, and they're cheerleaders for the strategy and product your company exhibits today. They help keep your current business. You aren't looking to them to help you redefine it, and this is true in B2C as well as B2B. As Henry Ford is rumored to have said, "If I had asked people what they wanted, they would have said faster horses." Achieving expertise about your industry and customer base, recognizing how to transfer technologies from one industry to the other, and understanding how to build successful relationships with customers are admirable skills, but they're wholly insufficient to survive in the Connected World. The forming ecosystems in the Connected World will look starkly different from the ones in existence today. The role of your firm in it may also change. Suppliers, for example, may realize that they have most of the assets and capabilities necessary to disintermediate their customers from users further down the value chain. Look carefully for your future customer and put them in the center of your perspective. Design for the best experiences for them, and concentrate on the "adjacent industries" to smooth experiences.

DATA: THE CURRENCY OF THE CONNECTED WORLD

In determining the adjacent industries that matter, you want to start by identifying the customers you'll want to target in the future. Think about how they'll use the product or service you're providing, with the understanding that it may not necessarily be the end point of the value chain. Extending the value chain is a challenge for traditional companies whose only worry in the past was about how to get the product into the hands of consumers. It's even difficult for the internet's early pioneers.

Consider that almost everyone carries a map on his or her phone. A decade ago, that map would've cost money. It was sold as a software product. Occasionally, the map company would provide software updates, and they, too, cost money. In the intervening years, companies realized they were in a better position to monetize the information than the consumer who was actually generating the data. With this thought in mind, the mapmakers created an interesting transaction agreement with their users. Users don't have to pay with money. Instead, they will pay with the data they produce while using the map and even when they're not using it. The new goal of these companies was to get the software in as many hands as possible so they could create the largest network with the most nuanced and developed data. Data that would help make the map more accurate and provide value to new customers willing to pay for the information about users of the map.

The "network effects" products or services create will raise the consumer's awareness of the producing companies, but it may not be how the company makes its profit. Monetization also happens on the platform economics level, when companies can sell the aggregated data to other players for advertising or strategic planning. Companies want to know the daily habits of current and potential customers. Do they combine certain types of errands? What's the weather like when they go shopping? What types of transportation do they take? A company with a map on the phones of consumers can provide answers to all of these questions. Again, it's about putting the human in the middle and looking at all the devices and nondevices that surround him or her in order to get a better sense of the person's total experience. We don't say these companies are in the mapping software business. Information generation, analysis, and brokering are what they now do. Although this monetization strategy is common in the digital world, it will likely be ubiquitous when competing in the Connected World. It's a perfect example of the economic patterns discussed in chapter 2, and it shows how users and customers can be two distinct groups in the Connected World.

DEVELOP COMPREHENSIVE PERSONAS

Almost a decade ago, we worked on a white paper for the automotive industry. The idea was to evaluate how the connected vehicle would impact the industry. When we examined automotive company value chains that were being designed for their connected products, they were too familiar-looking. They started with a vehicle design, which they then took over to engineering. Next, manufacturing would assemble the vehicle from raw materials and the components they got from suppliers. Finished assembling the vehicle, they'd roll it off and send it to the showroom. The standard industry value chains still had large chevrons with "sales," "after-sales and services," and "resale and disposal" listed on them. We dug into these areas more deeply to find automotive companies were still viewing the connected vehicle as a product. When we created and studied customer touchpoint maps for our automotive clients, most still had fifty to one hundred touchpoints that included traditional media (e.g., TV, radio, print), digital and social media (e.g., website, microsite, Facebook, etc.), and traditional product sales stages (e.g., showroom, test drive, call center, etc.). During ownership of the product, they had only traditional service touchpoints mapped out, such as warranty repair, roadside assistance, and off-lease campaigning. The average new car owner shops for a car every three to five years. These touchpoints were not unusual for the Unconnected World, where the only way to get a sense of the daily usage of the product was through survey, on a website, or at the dealership during a repair.

Leaders need to understand that the Connected World presents the opportunity for a paradigm shift in customer relationships. The most important touchpoint in the Connected World is the product itself (or the point of service consumption for service companies). Connected products and services will give you the ability to understand the who, what, where, when, why, and how of a consumer using your product. Certain sensors may even allow you to watch or monitor the product or customers when it's in use, learning which other connections are being used at the same time. Once you have that footprint of how your product is being used with other ones, you can begin designing a more relevant product, one that works seamlessly for that specific user. The information isn't working to improve the product. Rather, it's working to improve the ecosystem and eventually the user's life.

Because it becomes all about context, it's critical you observe and understand adjacent businesses so you can design your product and service with them in mind and form unique relationships to enhance the user experience. If you're a car company that expects your vehicle to work seamlessly with a city's infrastructure, you may have to work out agreements with municipalities and road commissions to exchange data. You may ask the city to provide information regarding traffic lights. In return, the city will ask you to send back the coordinates when drivers ride over potholes.

For years, companies have created general personas to be used with marketing departments designing campaigns to reach prospective customers. Many companies have created customer relationship management (CRM) systems to track real customer information. Typically, such databases contained basic data about each individual customer. Companies used the information to build relationships or track information about purchases. Slowly, companies realized that with additional research they could move from demographics to psychographics, focusing more on people's interests, patterns, and lifestyles. For the most part, however, CRM information is still divorced from how people use products or consume services, and therefore insufficient in the Connected World. Traditionally, personas have been used to design, engineer, produce, and support products or processes. This method has been focused on the masses, or "classes" of customers. This will all change as companies plan on competing in the Connected World.

UNIQUE PERSON, UNIQUE PRODUCT

As sensors continue to be embedded in products to produce data in real time, this product-in-use data will be harvested to tell companies about the relationship people have with their products. Are people getting maximum benefit out of the product? Are they using it correctly? What is their surrounding environment like when using the product? Does the person use it early in the morning or late at night? Do they use it at home, in the office, or both? Does configuration and integration look different at home than it does at work? The richness of the true customer relationship management will intensify when firms have a much better understanding of how the product is in use. All of this provides an opportunity for firms to offer environment integrations, offering choices to customers, or tips on how to use the product based on past usage of the specific users and others with similar personas. Services are starting to collect information about users even when the product isn't actively in use in order to prepare to be more relevant when they are used.

Uber, for example, is known to continue collecting data on users after they leave the car and have stopped using the service. What it's doing is looking for patterns in order to enhance the travel experience of its users, which it doesn't believe ends when the user gets out of the vehicle. It's looking to provide transportation-relevant services all the way to the person's end destination. If the person is dropped at a street corner, the company wants to know if he or she will go straight into a building or walk another block. It's not about simply understanding the user when they summon the vehicle, or when they're physically inside it. It wants to learn what's relevant to the person following its usage, or beyond. Maybe it'll build a persona of a customer who window shops for ten minutes before entering the final destination, or makes a stop at the grocery store before heading home at night. Uber can see where people shop, as well as the stores that don't interest them. It can use this information to build partnerships and services that are meaningful to this persona, as it did with services such as Uber Eats.

Another question you'll want answered is whether those brands that are part of the person's lifestyle can be seamlessly integrated into your product or service. In the early 1990s, Ford Motor Company came out with an Eddie Bauer edition for several of its vehicles. They came in certain colors and had different fits and finishes. This type of affinity marketing was common, although it had mixed results.

Today, a company such as Stitch Fix is employing a persona-based integration form of affinity marketing to shake up the fashion industry. It has always fallen on the consumer or store clerk to mix and match apparel and assemble an outfit and wardrobe. This integration was accomplished by bringing several brands together based on how the human thought they matched. Stitch Fix, a clothing home delivery service, uses persona to match clothes for consumers—taking from multiple brands—and delivering it to their homes. Amazon is taking this mode a step further with its Echo Look. A connected device sits in the closet and takes full-length photographs of the user. Using machine learning and advice from fashion specialists, it will study the photo and evaluate whether the outfit is the right style for the user. It will also suggest other options and provide a way to make those purchases. Interactive logic is bringing many brands together.

If you're a senior leader, you may want to talk with the CIO about how the company's product connects to the customer data from a systems perspective. In most legacy companies, the product information system is probably managed separately from the customer data repository. After all, there was never a strong reason for them to be connected. This emerging data set of product-in-use data extends the relationship a company can have with its customers. It extends the role of customer relationship management and bridges the traditional customer and product data environments. Personalization will be a goal for the future, and product-in-use data will be the key to achieving it.

Transferring or significantly altering the legacy CRM and product systems could cost millions of dollars, but maybe now is the time to start thinking about investing in merging the two data sets. The world is slowly working toward segments of one, where companies will build personas around one customer using unique products.

It will be crucial from an IT perspective to have the ability to match customer records to a unique product ID. In some ways, it's no different than the auto industry having the ability to track customers to the individual cars they own or use through vehicle identification numbers (VINs). VINs are unique for each car, across all cars ever manufactured. This unique identification (such as VINs or serial numbers) has often been limited to expensive or complex products. In other industries, especially in batch industries, it's much more difficult to track each individual product. Instead, they have ever only identified a model and batch identifier for quality purposes, not for in-use observation. Your CIO in the Connected World will need the ability to identify, track, and manage each connected product, whether it's a wine bottle or a diaper.

Seamless and automatic integration becomes the real benefit of creating these ultrapersonalized customer records. Based on a history of past usage, a company that is aware of how its product is being used can take away the mental and physical effort required to start up the next service the person demands as part of the experience. It can be offered as a choice. Let's say you were to travel to the same city every two weeks for work. You stay at the same hotel, and after check-in you always head up to the room and order one of two dishes off the room service menu. There's enough data collected on you for your mobile device to know that once you've been driving fifty miles east on a Tuesday morning that you are off for your biweekly business trip. Theoretically, through quick swipes of your device, which is connected to the hotel, you can answer a series of questions that will speed up your check-in and deliver dinner to your room without having to stand at the front desk or sit on the telephone while they take down your order. This personalization of how you use the hospitality product will be an extension of your CRM record. It can be taken even further. As the hotel room itself is configurable, you may not walk into a hotel room but rather "your" hotel room. Lighting can be adjusted to your settings. TV stations can be sorted to your most watched, and on-screen information can be personalized for you. The connected bed can adjust firmness to your settings and report sleeping patterns back into your health applications. You'll even get a wake-up call the next morning, not at your "usual time" but customized based on the meetings on your calendar. This "personalization" service will configure the use of a product or service to be for you, not a class of you. This will make your life easier and allow you to make better use of your most scarce resource: time.

In a certain sense, we're already moving past the one-product-to-one-customer model. With ride and work sharing services, we are encountering a model of one product uniquely identified to many users, even if it's only one at a time. With certain ride sharing services, it may even be one product to many users at one time. This doesn't mean you're required to think about immediately jumping into this world. Still, it's important to understand the evolution so you can start taking small steps into this new landscape. If you're a car company, for example, looking at the autonomous vehicle, you may decide to focus on the persona of the daily commuter, as opposed to the vacationing family of four. You'll build the majority of your value around that ecosystem and treat the latter persona as the exception. There's the option to take the opposite approach and cater to the niche market of family experiences in an autonomous vehicle. Either way, the focus turns to the ecosystem and away from the language of branding. It's saying goodbye to a car company holding up a certain model as the green solution to the environmental persona, or the sports car that will answer the pains of the midlife crisis persona.

PERSONAS WILL INFORM THE ENTIRE COMPANY

Traditionally, marketing departments have developed personas to help describe groups of customer "types." They develop products, services, campaigns, and sales strategies to best fit these classes of people. What changes as we move into the connecting world is the need to move toward the ultrapersonal persona. Personas and customer information are no longer going to be used only by the marketing department but also by departments responsible for engineering and servicing (post-sale) the product. As firms take monetization strategies beyond the point of traditional product sales, it means the firm will need to be able to interact with each customer in a consistent way. You can consider this a Persona for One.

As your firm enters this ultrapersonal Connected World, the supply chain will extend beyond traditional retail and into the point of product usage and service experience. As the pace of innovation picks up, and as more brands and industries connect to your product and service, it will become more of a challenge to treat people as isolated classes, targets to hang up on the walls inside departments. Marketing will have little use for terms such as "soccer moms" or "millennials," which are classifications of groups, not of individuals using the product.

Inside many firms, a natural tension exists between the manufacturing and marketing groups. Manufacturing wants to build a product a certain way because it's operating in a world of constraints—budgets, capabilities, investment. Marketing, on the other hand, is interested in a product having utility and functionality that fits the customer. The product-in-use data from the Connected World offers a different lens regarding this tension. Information can flow in two directions, to and from the product. This new flow will help present new options for product management/marketing groups and engineering/manufacturing groups alike.

Regarding information flowing from the product, companies can now receive data about how products are used, which can lead to better design, reduce unused features, and drive marketing. Knowing how each customer thinks about and uses the product will likely allow a company to be more relevant to a consumer. The "product in use" will become king in terms of determining how to build, market, and sell the product. Whereas your company used to engage in inductive reasoning, assuming you had an idea of what the customer wanted, "product in use" data will now allow empirical evidence to drive functional strategies, with internal mandates of functional areas becoming subordinate to what the product-experience data is saying.

Information flowing to the product allows for a paradigm shift for the engineering and manufacturing functions in your firm. As updates can be sent to a product while it is "in use," a product can grow in relevancy to your customers. To allow this option, your product will need to be viewed as a platform, capable of getting "smarter" as it is used. This over-the-air (OTA) update capability will stress your engineering group to consider how to create a platform that will be somewhat future-proof. The bigger stress will likely be to your manufacturing function, which is used to focus on key performance indicators around getting high-quality products out of a final checkpoint in a plant. Now, manufacturing may extend into customers using products. Reflashing software versus creating hardware.

This evolution brings its challenges, such as figuring out how to align strategy, innovation, engineering, design, and all of the other functions with the actual objective data on customer usage. If the alignment doesn't take shape, you can count on a future of functional tensions bogging down your organization.

THE OTHER SIDE OF DATA TO CONSIDER

The data of how customers use products may end up informing the other teams in the organization, and this is especially true when it comes to the data about the product's own performance. We can look at there being two types of data, each one contributing, in the end, to higher functioning products (see figure 16). One of these sets of data being sent back from the product relates to how well the product is performing. This lower maturity usage of data rapidly informs current functions inside a company on how to increase quality, lower cost, and remove unnecessary features. It can help the design team and engineers produce more useful and efficient products.

Further, the company can learn a significant amount about the product to a degree that it can help make decisions about shifting the business model and offering services or moving into a different business altogether.

The second type of data speaks to how the user is experiencing the product. Here, the information isn't necessarily leading to major hardware redesign. The product-in-use (PiU) data is of a higher maturity. It's knowing the customer in ways the customer has never been known before, extending CRM beyond its current capabilities, and identifying top-line revenue opportunities versus cost out.

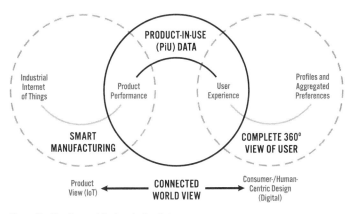

Figure 16 – Two Types of Product-in-Use Data.

It allows the engineers to configure the software for the specific user and enables marketing to reexamine its partner programs as part of an effort to enhance the user experience.

Different configurations of an existing product can serve up choices to the user that are consistent with the person's personality, preferences, and specific use cases for that time. Whether it's an autonomous vehicle driving differently based on who is the passenger or a hotel room configuring itself based on who has checked in, personalization relevancy will be a big part of making the connecting world deliver on its promise.

As personalization and configuration in the cloud deepens and as alliance management gathers information from other touchpoints, we will see user preferences used in even more logical ways. Say a customer has a smart home and is a member of a hotel chain with smart technologies. Now, when this customer checks into the hotel, the room's air conditioner, lighting, and bed are set according to his or her preferences that have been observed in his or her own home. The preferred television stations come up on the screen right when the guest hits the remote, saving the person from scrolling through a long list. His or her favorite beers are in the room's mini fridge, cooled to the right temperature. Generating usage information can be configured to other products and services in the user's life. As vehicles become automated, there will be a push to turn them into a living room or office on wheels. Manufacturers aren't collecting data just for their products. Rather, it's so the manufacturer, and other OEMs consuming the same information, can become more relevant in the consumer's life.

Even if you're not currently a customer-centric organization, or feel that you'll never be able to make the turn in the future and will always stay a product company, it doesn't mean you can avoid the Connected World. It's impossible to take the position that you'll continue to exist as a distinctive product company. Further, there are incredible opportunities to improve your products based on usage data. The first step is to open up your architecture and allow sensors to be embedded in your products or coordinated with sensors in your customers' assortment of mobile devices.

ADOPTING A BROADER PERSPECTIVE

The Connected World demands that businesses adopt a broader and more targeted perspective. Leaders have to first ask if they're even going to be in the same business, and if so, how they will compete and participate as a company that expands past the discrete functionality their product offers. It's obvious that internal discussions and decisions on how to develop the necessary capabilities to bridge them to the Connected World will have to take place. A company will have to decide whether to build the capabilities themselves or buy them from an outside party. There are many legitimate considerations, and any decision needs to harmonize with the company's financial situation. All these decisions, however, must start with a perspective of how the product or service will engage in the Connected World. PiU data will become the core basis from which all of your decisions are eventually made, and the need to make decisions will be constant.

A complex product industry like automotive plans ahead seven years for models, and maybe two-and-a-half to three years for major feature releases inside the vehicles. Those life cycles may no longer be sufficiently frequent, especially if some manufacturers understand ways to engineer on-demand feature enhancements into software, even without the request of the customer. If you're not thinking about the direct correlation between product life cycles and PiU data, you are potentially missing the very thing that will preserve the viability of your company.

Further, your ability to handle the PiU data is crucial. This means gaining the capabilities to capture, manage, and analyze the tremendous amounts of generated data. It's this skill that will allow your organization to find meaningful patterns so it can adjust product life cycles and share the data with the other players in the ecosystem. The capabilities to manage personas and segment the data are unique.

Those with deep pockets and available resources can invest in building these new capabilities. They may also play a future role in the negotiations around how to get persona data into this stream of data that forms new ecosystems.

Companies that don't have sufficient prominence or the internal slack resources to build the new capabilities are going to be left determining how they can negotiate the best deal to keep themselves as some part of the future Connected World, which is a risky position. Put simply, they won't have the option to decide how they want their companies to participate. In some industries, persona management companies may already be a step ahead of you. They'll already know what their customers want, and they'll tell your company what they expect from it. Maybe these new entrants will come with a data model they're looking to extend, or are interested in rolling up products into their ecosystem. If you want to survive, then you'll be forced to accept their terms over the role your product company will play.

Firms that don't feel as if they have sufficient differentiation opportunity in their products to compete in the future have to decide what business they're going to be in. This doesn't mean liquidate the company and send everyone home with a check. All it means is that the time has come to signal openness to strategic discussions.

DEVELOP NEW STRATEGIES

"Strategy without tactics is the slowest route to victory.
Tactics without strategy is the noise before defeat."

—SUN TZU

We've discussed that speed to market during periods of discontinuity is crucial. It establishes position and awareness in the marketplace and allows a company to start building its role in the alliances forming the new connected ecosystem. Formulating new strategies is a critical step of making a fast transformation; however, it can also be a great source of delay for most companies.

The emergence of the Connected World will be such a dramatic change to the competitive environment that it will force executives to reconsider the purpose of their firms. This isn't familiar territory. Organizations, after all, excel at executing. They aren't inherently reflective or built to question purpose. Humans on the other hand, for the most part, are inclined to ask such questions. Visit any company's lunchroom and sit with some of the employees for fifteen minutes. They'll tell you everything that's wrong with the company, and how they'd improve it if they were put in a leadership position immediately. Oddly, the company, which in many ways is simply the sum of all those human reflections, can't reflect because it requires some way to weigh the options and form a structured consensus. We've already discussed the persistence of the dominant logic in the minds of executives and employees that can delay the recognition that "this time, it really is different."

What follows in this chapter are reflections and tools to be used in creating a structured way to internally think about and discuss strategic options for your firm. Stand at the edge of your company and take a 360-degree gaze. Look at your industry and adjacent ones to understand external market forces. These are the ones that will affect you and all other firms. Treat your company like a "black box" as you consider these market dynamics. Standing at that same edge, you can turn around and look inward at the internal forces at work in your own organization. These forces will signal how ready your firm is to participate in, shape, or be shaped by the external forces. It's at this critical inside out juncture that your transformation will truly be planned.

STRATEGY 101

We have found it helpful to discuss strategy in three hierarchical layers. The hierarchy helps because it implies sequencing of the strategic decisions. The distinct layers of strategy—corporate, business, and functional, as seen in figure 17—focus the discussion to a single domain of the overall strategy. The hierarchy prescribes a top-down sequence in the consideration of strategy. Each layer of the strategy is intended to answer a single simple question asked by an outside individual to a leader inside the firm.

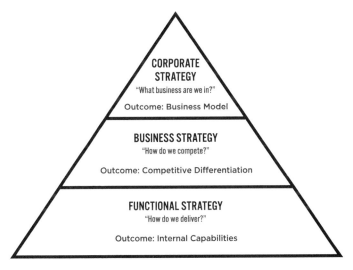

Figure 17 – Layers of Firm Strategy

WHAT BUSINESS ARE YOU IN?

Corporate strategy is the top layer of the strategic hierarchy. The purpose of the corporate strategy is to position the company in a specific market by trying to answer the following question: "What business are you in?" Through answering this question, leaders will understand the organization's mission and value proposition. It specifies the intended value of the firm to the market and implicitly defines the customer groups the firm will serve both now and in the future. The main deliverable generated by a firm's corporate strategy effort is the firm's business model.

The corporate strategy defines the most fundamental level of identity for the firm, and it also determines how broadly the executives of the firm envision the firm's future. For example, a firm could identify itself either as an automotive manufacturing company or a mobility company. An automotive manufacturing company would seem to be limited to dealing with the production of cars, whereas a firm defining itself as a mobility firm may be currently producing cars but is ready to consider broadening its offering to include services that have to do with moving people, goods, and even information. This simple shift may even set the firm on a journey to leave the manufacturing of vehicles to a supplier organization.

Using a different industry as an example, an executive could be asked, "Are you a map company, or is your company focused on monetizing information about people's mobility?" Ty Beltramo, the former CTO of MapQuest and former chief architect at OnStar, often speaks about modern-day mapping solution companies. He explains that the location-based services "in-use data" can be broader than just a single transaction. Say a GPS map is helping route a driver heading to Home Depot. Suddenly, the driver changes course and decides to head to Lowe's. This type of data is useful to both Home Depot and Lowe's. Both companies will want to know how often it happens and try to discern from other data points whether there is a clear explanation for the behavior. This type of information can have a major impact on strategy and investment. So to an external observer, MapQuest might be considered a map provider, but to the insiders, it's a mobility data management company creating services for third-party firms about the behavior of its map users. In the end, they are monetizing user information from a broad user group. They have created a two-sided marketplace using the map and routing services to attract a large user population, while monetizing information about those who use the service.

HOW DO YOU COMPETE?

Business strategy is the second layer of strategy and answers the question, "How do you compete?" A firm's business strategy explains the general pattern by which a firm's products and services are intended to be differentiated from those of competitors in the same or similar business models. Maybe you'll decide to be a low-price provider like Southwest Airlines, or you might have decided to differentiate in an area other than price, charging a premium price for a higher level of service, a product with more features, or a service with a more sophisticated customer treatment experience, such as the Ritz-Carlton hotels. Alternatively, maybe your firm will focus on the unique needs of a particular segment of the market and cater your product or service offering to this niche market, like Winnebago does with its motor homes, a highly specialized portion of the automobile market. Business strategy, like corporate strategy, is an externally focused intention, although with a shorter time horizon. A firm's executives wrestle with the issues of differentiation on a regular basis, seeking to find ways to create some customer-perceived advantage over competitors. While there may be regular ongoing adjustments to the business strategy, such as price discounts or specials, the basic business strategies of low price, high quality, and niche functionality are themselves generally long lasting with a firm.

Business strategy is perhaps the most nuanced layer of the strategy model. Patterns of "how you compete" are not always easily observable, although if understood, they can help make investment criteria much more straightforward.

The digitization of a company's business may be about efficiencies in order to keep up with market pressures, or it may be about differentiation in a market, making it a core tenant of the business strategy. Our friend Jeff Poiner leads digital health and IT innovation for one of the world's largest health-care providers, which, like many health systems, traditionally has provided acute care. Through the deployment of IoT devices across the traditional acute care environment, Jeff is reshaping the firm's business strategy and allowing for efficiencies to be realized. Placing these devices in the homes of patients will redefine the health-care experience and allow the firm to compete differently from its competitors. It will offer more personal and relevant services in environments that are nontraditional, such as patients' homes.

HOW DO YOU DELIVER?

Functional strategy makes up the final layer of firm strategy. It answers the core question, "How do you deliver?" It's the one layer of strategy focused on internal capabilities required to deliver the business and corporate strategies. The implementation of the functional strategy results in the internal operation of the firm, including the oversight of external suppliers that serve to extend internal capabilities.

In addition to defining the portfolio of internal capabilities, the functional strategy also prescribes the allocation of internal resources (human and financial capital) to develop and mature the firm's capabilities. Resource allocation is done in a manner that reflects the executive's perspective of the relative importance of that capability to the success of the firm and its importance to the realization of business and corporate strategies. Capabilities that are considered important get the resources required to ensure they are fully enabled. Less important capabilities get fewer resources. The internal structure (processes, systems, policies, and organizational hierarchy) and enabling resources (employees and budget) are the components of capabilities and the means by which firms deliver on business and corporate strategies. In the first decade of this century, for example, global discrete manufacturing companies typically invested between 2 and 4 percent of their revenue in internal information technology (IT). During this era, the role of IT was generally considered to be a necessity to operate a manufacturing business. A necessary evil, if you will, but not the source of any competitive advantage. In the Connected World, however, leaders are beginning to see the role of IT expanding significantly as product companies need to better manage data about the customer, new connected services, and how the products are used. In this connecting world, IT will switch from being a necessary evil to a source for innovation. IT functions are likely responsible for managing the digital business innovation life cycle. Accordingly,

IT budgets as a percentage of overall revenue will rise to deliver on these new capabilities needed to support the externally facing strategies.

We have tried to describe the strategy layers in a way that makes the interdependence obvious. "What business are you in?" "How do you compete?" and "How do you deliver?" Executives should understand how these questions align and that deliberate adjustments to one layer must take into consideration the potential necessary adjustments to the others.

Every firm operates with these three layers of strategy to deliver the current operating results. Not every firm makes each of the strategy layers explicit, and it isn't necessary to do so. If the firm is performing well and the industry is stable, making the strategies explicit and reviewing the alignment among them may be a low priority for executives who feel nothing ever changes. However, if the firm executives intend to continue to do well in the emerging connecting world, it's imperative to revisit the three layers of strategy from the top down. In the next sections, we will walk you through some reflection of reexamining the basic building blocks for a "Connected Strategy." We'll discuss some emerging models that already exist at the corporate strategy layer and then analyze the implications at the business and functional strategy layers. Our discussion is only the tip of the iceberg of options and implications, but we think you'll start to see that this time is truly different.

NEW CORPORATE STRATEGY OPTIONS

What business will you be in after the world connects? In order to answer this question, you must reflect on what markets will exist in which to compete. This isn't easy, as markets are still forming; however, there are enough patterns emerging to start placing bets now. As discussed in chapter 2, the merger of industrial economics with information economics is creating the crucible for new emerging business models. Products will take advantage of the PiU data that can create new product features, create new services for the user, inform experiences, or simply provide relevant information to the product owner, manufacturer, or service provider. This new steady stream of information will allow for ultrapersonalization of how a product works and services perform. Additionally, this PiU data will allow for users to be grouped into distinct communities based on usage patterns. These usage groups can become the basis of generating additional revenue from third parties who pay for access to the community, or for insights about the community. The result is the creation of what will become one of the dominant business models of the Connected World: the two-sided platform.

Deciding what business you'll want to be in will likely revolve around the following questions:

- Will you decide to offer a connected experience, or supply a product or service to a company that does? (B2B Supplier)
- Will you offer connected products, services informed from connected products, or both? (How complete of a set of services will you offer, and how important will products be to the strategy?)
- If you offer your connected experiences to the end user, will you solely monetize PiU data to the users (Connected Features or User Services) or will you develop a two-sided platform that has distinct users and separate customers who buy access or insights about the users?

Your options for your future corporate strategy will likely differ depending on if you lead an existing product company or a digital service firm. The basic shift for a digital services firm is dependent on how much of its digital service experience needs to be informed through connected products and connected environments (sensored infrastructures). If it's determined that a large part of what you want to offer to the market is related to connected products associated with your service, or your services are significantly dependent on the environments in which they are offered, then you may wish to offer more than just services, perhaps offering your service through a product. You will want to consider how the end user will gain access to the product, and how you will gain access to information from the environment. Will your firm leverage other firms' products or produce your own, and what type of partnerships will be necessary to gain access to complete ecosystems of information?

If you are a current product company leader, the business you'll be in could vary even more than that of your digital service firm counterpart. You'll be coming from the "T" side of the IoT mash-up. Knowing if you want to be a product company, a service company, or both will depend significantly on whether your future customer needs your product to get the experience you offer. If not, it's likely you'll use connected information to provide differentiating services through one of the business model options that we explore in the following pages. Without this, you'll likely become the leader of a commodity supplier. The business models we explore apply to firms regardless of where they begin the journey. Both digital service and product companies will require considerations of the question, "What business are you in?" As you review the potential business model building blocks, you'll need to bring your business's lens to them to consider how they fit with your current reality.

OPTION 1: REMAIN UNCONNECTED AND SUPPLY THE CONNECTED COMPANIES

Some legacy product companies will remain unconnected as the connecting world emerges. Sometimes this will be by executive choice, sometimes because of an inability to access the necessary capabilities, and other times because of a failure to create a compelling service offering. Choosing to remain unconnected likely means accepting to not have a deep relationship with the end user or consumer. In the Connected World, few products will be completely unconnected, so companies that decide not to aggressively connect their products will likely be relegated to becoming a B2B supplier to companies that offer a connected experience. This means their products will likely be sold to another company, potentially in a white-label capacity, and then eventually offered to an end user or consumer.

This can already be witnessed in certain transforming industries. We often use the automotive to mobility industry shift as an example because of the massive and easily identifiable disruption taking place. Digital service players such as Google/Alphabet have been testing the B2B supplier relationship for the last few years. This digital firm has become a supplier to the auto industry, providing software and media services of their own through the car. Although the monetization strategies differ from many traditional OEM-to-supplier relationships, these early deals for Android Auto fit easily into the automotive industry's typical supplier patterns. What is much more interesting is Alphabet's (Google's parent company) Waymo division's relationship with automotive companies. In these instances, automotive OEMs such as Chrysler are providing special-order vehicles to the digital service providers, who are outfitting them with additional sensors and software, branding them Waymo, and providing an on-demand autonomous rideshare service in certain markets. In this instance, the automotive company becomes a supplier to the digital services firm.

OPTION 2: OFFER A FULL CONNECTED EXPERIENCE TO YOUR CUSTOMERS

All firms will need to eventually come to grips with the fact that they must compete in the connecting world, and that connected products and informed services and experiences are key to relevancy. Leaders must evaluate their firm's role in markets that will be built on economic principles that are no longer simply industrial or information but rather both. Step 1 is to understand this and create scenarios about how their current or future products could be embedded with, or take advantage of, sensors, which would potentially generate future usage-based services. When dealing with clients who are early in the First Mile, still trying to determine the disruptive potential of the connected technologies, we pose the following questions: If your product could talk about itself when it is being used, what would it say? Who would be interested in listening? What value would that be? If the product could listen, what information would it most seek and why? If your service could learn from its environment, which things would it talk to? From these basic questions, a firm can start to consider the types of sensors to embed in their products, such as what attributes of the product's readiness or in-use readings it will measure. Then they can build use cases about the service potential of the data collected or accessed. This begins the discussion internally about creating services from product usage. It's baby steps, yet effective ones.

In order to offer the connected experience to their users, firms will likely need to offer products that can sense how they are being used and performing. These "products" will need to be more of a platform with real-time customization that can dynamically react to input from the user, the environment, and the brand. Additionally, they will need to offer services through the product. These intelligent or "smart" digital services will bring additional value to the consumer and potentially differentiate the firm's business toward the customer.

A simplified graphic outlines this business model in figure 18. You can see in this depiction that in the end a firm has to choose whether to buy products or services from a different firm (option 1) or to build out all the necessary capabilities to become a Connected Experience Firm. Regardless of the sourcing approach, the business model is primarily the same. The firm is offering a complete connected experience to the customer, who is also the user. Value needs to be derived from the user to cover the costs of producing and managing the product, as well as supporting the services surrounding it. There's an opportunity to build a partnership between brands that offer related but different products and services to the same customers. (This will be discussed in the Symbiotic Partnership section that follows.)

CORE CUSTOMER: PRODUCT/SERVICE USERS

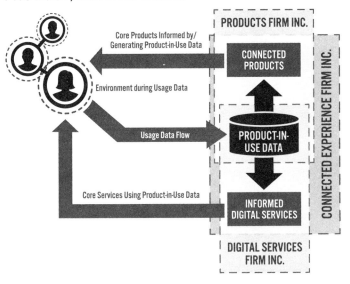

Figure 18 – One-Sided Connected Business Model Options.

OPTION 3: OFFER A CONNECTED EXPERIENCE AND BUILD A TWO-SIDED PLATFORM BUSINESS

Perhaps the most discussed business model in the Connected World will be that of the two-sided platform. Due to popular success with digital service firms such as Waze, Airbnb, and Google, many consumer-facing digital service firms seek ways to monetize not only their core product or service but also the information they collect about their users. A navigation services provider that gives its maps and routings away for "free" completely shifts the landscape for the navigation services industry. On the surface, this shift seems to be a business strategy conversation. There are two companies both providing navigation services and digital maps, and one is competing as the "low cost" provider. The real difference, however, may be that they are not in the same business at all. A firm, such as Google or Waze, trades the map and the navigation service for access to the user's information. The user doesn't pay with monetary value but instead allows for Google to monetize his information in ways that he as an individual would never be able to. Google then turns around, aggregates the information, and sells insights to companies that want to know about the user or classes thereof. Here, we have two similar offerings to the users—or side 1 of the market—but two entirely different business models.

The most basic of corporate strategy considerations for

firms is already, and will continue to be, how much of a two-sided platform model for their products can exist. How much of each side do they want to own, and how much can they afford to own? Affordability is measured in the pseudocurrency of the capabilities necessary to create and manage both sides of the platform. (This will be discussed in more detail in chapter 6.) The Technical Discontinuity to Industry Disruption model shown earlier (chapter 1) describes this dilemma. The creation of new industry business models creates the requirement to review the firm's strategies. The following paragraph describes the options for business leaders in a deeper manner.

Side 1 of the business model is the user. This user can pay for the product or services in any number of ways that include a one-time financial payment, in the form of an ongoing subscription or as-used fee, or by allowing companies access to their information about how they consume a product or service. Side 2 consists of many different types of third-party users that find value in the information generated from side 1 users and captured by the two-sided company platform. We show this in figure 19.

A firm that manages to retain autonomy over these side 1 core offerings establishes access control to the user-customer. The combined control of both the core data services (side 1) and the second-order services (side 2) creates the full economic potential of the two-sided platform model. It allows firms to choose from a number of business model alternatives about where, when, and from whom to collect revenue. This creates flexibility when it comes to the pricing of both products and services. The two-sided model allows firms to decide to offer core services at no charge to side 1 users in order to generate consumption of the service and rapidly expand the volume of usage data that can then be used to generate revenue from the side 2 market of third-party firms. This has been a successful model for many digital firms to create a community of active identifiable users that can be then used to create second-order data usage offerings.

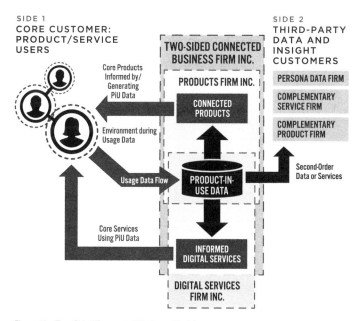

Figure 19 – Two-Sided Connected Business Model.

Two-sided platform business models are actually not new and not a creation of the digital world. If you can recall the pre-credit card era and the concept of traveler's checks from providers such as American Express and Thomas Cook, then you're recalling a two-sided platform. Financial services firms offered traveler's checks as a form of secure, refundable, pseudocurrency. People traveling to foreign countries need not worry about carrying cash. They could carry traveler's checks and redeem them with participating foreign retailers for goods and services. If they were lost or stolen, the traveler could be issued replacements without any loss of value. To launch traveler's checks as a service, American Express had to create two markets, or the two sides of the platform. Side 1 was the market of travelers looking for protection from loss or theft of cash. Side 2 was the market of foreign retailers seeking to sell to travelers and willing to accept the traveler's checks, which could be redeemed back with American Express for payment. Both sides of the model were necessary to make the platform viable, and American Express had to develop both of them simultaneously. American Express dealt with a chicken-and-egg problem of which side of the platform to develop first. Side 1 or side 2? The answer seems to be that they needed to be developing both sides together. It was a somewhat complicated business model with significant risk associated with the speed at which each side of the platform was developed.

Fast forward to the internet era, where leveraging the principles of information economics as applied to digital applications has enhanced the two-sided platform. More than a decade ago, Apple introduced the iPhone along with its App Store concept. iPhone created the side 1 community of users that consume the various native iPhone applications. The App Store concept became a place where app developers could offer their services (apps), thereby becoming the side 2 market. Apple created both markets and controlled access to side 1 and created the architectural standards to control the nature of the app services on side 2. Apple controls and manages both sides of the platform and has created network effects on both sides to accelerate the growth of each market and the value of the overall platform. It charges for the devices and some services to the side 1 users, and it takes a percentage of each sale that side 2 companies make to their side 1 users.

There are plenty of examples of two-sided business models in the increasingly connecting world. Facebook is a two-sided model where side 1 is more than two billion users, and side 2 is the companies that advertise on the platform. Users don't pay with money. Instead, they offer access to their data that Facebook then monetizes to the side 2 customers.

Airbnb is the all-time greatest disruptor to the hospitality business. This relatively new entrant places a major emphasis on its relationship with customers and brand loyalty, even though it doesn't own a single hotel room and, therefore, doesn't have any control over property. Other people own and maintain the properties, such as individuals or small business owners whose property typically sits unoccupied. Airbnb exploited the excess capacity in short-term unused private residential living space and built a two-sided platform model by connecting guests (side 1 users) to property owners (side 2 marketplace). Once it figured out the point of differentiation, it cut out everything else, giving up control in all other areas of a guest's stay. The guests bring their own bags to the room. No food is provided. At the end of the day, it's the same business as hotels but without the overhead.

Waze, which we discussed earlier in the book, is similar. The Waze community uses and actually adds content to the navigation product. This platform returns value to the users by helping them get from point A to point B in the most efficient manner. Monetarily speaking, Waze is a free application. The price point of free is logical considering the potential of network effects. The more users on the Waze network, the more valuable the network is to every current user and the more attractive the service is to future users. The user growth curve is exponential. Users instead pay by offering their usage data back to the Waze data repository. In the aggregate, and through analysis, the members of the Waze community answer indirectly a variety of questions about transportation and shopping habits. Waze analytics can develop a data-based point of view on questions of interest to third parties such as how far people will travel to buy groceries and whether they will drive out of their way to buy cheaper gas. By using the app, members of the community agree to allow Waze to broker the sale of this information to other companies. Google bought the company for $1.3 billion because of the seemingly endless possibilities for monetization of this data with the side 2 market. Two-sided platforms are here to stay and will be a key element of the basis of competition in the Connected World.

There is great potential to craft new business models that can propel a product firm into the Connected World using a two-sided platform model. The choice depends a great deal on firm-specific factors such as the current demand for the core product, the capability of the firm to generate compelling side 1 core usage services, and capability to manage the side 2 market for second-order data and services. We believe that two-sided platforms will likely become the default corporate strategy option for most firms in a product industry because of the autonomy it allows firms. However, as we have discussed previously, choosing the option and successfully delivering are quite different. The product firm choosing this option is going to need to treat legacy customers as users, and they're going to need to learn to get near real-time access to their behaviors. This isn't a natural phenomenon for product companies and introduces an entirely new level of managerial complexity. Two-sided platforms aren't easy either. Building side 1 costs time and money, and even though the firm's leaders can see the value for the side 2 users and side 2 data consumers, the market can be slow to appreciate the value until the model becomes proven.

BUILDING SYMBIOTIC PARTNERSHIPS

Some leaders will not be comfortable with relegating their firm to a supplier for a connected service or experience company. Others will doubt their ability to make the transformation to being a complete Connected Experience Firm, regardless if the platform is one-sided (users as customers) or two-sided (users and third-party customers). Continuing along a logical continuum, some companies with large populations of users or distinct differentiations in the market could choose to create market-facing symbiotic partnerships. Instead of having a digital services firm consume the unconnected product, or the unconnected product consume a third-party digital service capability, some firms may seek to form exclusive partnerships. This means the product company still sells its product directly to the end consumer, and the services firm provides its service directly to the end consumer. In this type of arrangement, a symbiosis partnership might be formed between a product firm that is unwilling or unable to create the necessary internal capabilities to connect its product and a digital service firm unwilling or unable to create the physical products. The result is two firms from separate industries—one from the things industry and one from the internet industry—partnering to enhance each of their service offerings.

Building a symbiotic partnership may be an effective way for product firms with lower level prominence in their current industry, and maybe without deep pockets, to navigate their way into the Connected World. The obvious advantage to the product firm is a low-cost and nonobtrusive way to enhance its product offering with connected services. The disadvantage, however, is giving up some control of the customer to the third-party service provider. The product company will no longer have full autonomy in the relationship with its user customers. The relationship will now be shared with the digital services firm. Further, depending on the level of customer demand for the unconnected product alone, the product firm may have limited influence in negotiating the potential revenue-sharing model with the data services company. Consequently, when, as we have predicted, the future value of a product becomes disproportionately weighted toward the product usage data services created, and away from the discrete product itself, the producers of the unconnected products will be easily substituted and, therefore, potentially cut out of that service revenue stream. The risk for the unconnected product company is that no matter how much they fight for a strong partnership, declining margins and market shift will constantly push them back to becoming a mere hardware provider to the digital service firm that will eventually take over some or all of the customer relationship. Many product firms may be forced into situations where the initial symbiotic relationship with a digital services firm changes over time when the digital services firm gains greater leverage over the financial results of the product company and can drain the profitability out of the host product business.

Even the strongest unconnected product brands that decide not to launch their own connected offering are likely to observe attempts by other third-party digital service companies to pull those unconnected products into their own service platform. The first wave of that activity may be third-party digital service firms looking to engineer a way to attach sensors to the product, possibly as an after-market accessory or using the sensors in a consumer's own mobile phone as a substitute for embedded sensors in the product. Through "hacking" the unconnected product, the third-party digital service firm could then begin to stream PiU data and convert that into services available for consumption by either the original product owners or other interested third-party service providers. For years, there has been discussion about "smart appliances," such as washing machines and refrigerators that connect to the internet to self-diagnose as well as automatically replenish goods used with the appliance. The large, capital-intense appliance industry has yet to dive deep into this connected offering and is likely incubating smaller services. Amazon, a digital services behemoth, decided not to wait. Instead of creating a competitive appliance, they decided to simply allow for consumers to "hack" their own appliances. Consumers can now stick the Amazon Dash button on their appliances and press the reorder button when they need to order more detergent. In the future, the washing machine may do this itself, but for now, Amazon has found a way to bypass the slower-moving appliance OEMs and begin cementing itself in the connected value chain, making future negotiations with product companies easier.

Firms that choose to partner with digital service firms, and even some that don't, will have an ongoing risk that service providers will take over the customer relationship. Only some product firms with unique products and strong brand appeal will likely survive but not mainstream products. There is still a small collector market for vinyl records in the era of streaming music, although there's no collector market for eight-track or cassette tape technologies. Few unconnected product firms will have the opportunity to find a niche home in the "retro" collector market.

Firms considering a partnership as a conscious strategic

choice are advised to be active in searching for a symbiotic partner with particular focus on negotiating the best partnership arrangements possible. Coming to a quick decision before competitors act will be critical. It's unlikely that there will be an excess of internet service firms for every product industry. Those product firms that run the First Mile the fastest are likely to have a better opportunity to establish the more favorable partnership terms with digital service firms. The ones that delay lose leverage and will lose autonomy over their future.

OPTION 4: SERVICE-ONLY AND AGGREGATED SERVICES PLATFORM FOR CONNECTED EXPERIENCES

As more and more two-sided business models take hold, and second-side economics stabilize, more service-only or service aggregation models will emerge as the product becomes commoditized. Some existing product firms may choose to move past the dependency on product as a revenue source and become committed to generating revenue almost exclusively from services and the enablement of connected experiences. This option would be a completely new business model for a legacy product company. It would need to transition from being a company collecting all or some revenue from the sale of product to collecting revenue exclusively from the sale of usage data services. There are precedents, prior to the Connected World, of firms founded as product firms that morphed over time into service firms. IBM, founded as International Business Machines, for more than half a century was the market leader in typewriters, then later in computers of various forms. Eventually, IBM divested all of its product business to become a services company.

General Electric's jet engine division manufactures engines laden with sensors that monitor the performance of engine components. GE determined that this enabled it to predict component problems and intercede with maintenance to prevent engine outages. Using this capability to keep its engines operating, GE morphed from being a provider of engines to a provider of engine uptime for aircraft companies. The GE revenue model switched from selling a jet engine product to selling thrust as a service. The clients of GE engines no longer have to pay for a capital asset. Instead, they pay for the guarantee of engine output as an expense.

There's also the example of Silicon Valley software companies developing autonomous driving solutions for automobiles. One option for these companies is to stay software service companies and partner with an existing automobile OEM to offer solutions integrated into existing auto OEMs, or only a single exclusive OEM. The second choice is directly selling an autonomous operating system that various OEMs have been certified to utilize. Alternatively, there is the question of whether these software companies choose to become producers of their own automobiles embedded with their autonomous driving operating systems. This would place them as both a product and a service company.

At the same time, a number of the largest automotive OEMs have signaled through press releases and investments that they're also developing autonomous driving software solutions to embed in their future vehicles. PiU data will be the basis for future services, and they'll think about digital platform models as a means to monetize usage data. In effect, the largest OEMs currently seem motivated to expand from product companies to product and service companies. For the big members of any major information or industrial industry cluster, the goal could be to become product and service companies, and eventually just connected experience companies.

Product firms that follow the steps of IBM or the GE Aerospace Division are committing to this option 4 corporate strategy. As they morph into a services company, they'll have some additional considerations to ponder. If they no longer generate revenue from products but only use products as a platform to generate service revenue, they should review whether to fully outsource the manufacturing of their product. Legacy product firms that consider this option may find that releasing the financial capital currently tied up in the assets dedicated to product creation may allow them to invest in enhancing the connected service offering, which will mean their morphing from product to service companies.

In figure 20, the Digital Service and Data Aggregation Firm has chosen option 4 and is now offering product firms A and B the chance to join into its data services ecosystem. The Digital Service and Data Aggregation firm expands its service revenue opportunity across the industry and builds larger communities of service users that can become a source of service revenue from firm A and B product users, some of which may be partly shared between the firms. Additionally, in such an expanded scale model, the Digital Service and Data Aggregation Firm would have a much more robust repository of usage data to be offered to the second-order market of third-party firms. This would, of course, be a potential increase in the revenue for the service firm.

Option 4 is in many ways a modified version of the Symbiotic Partner model for the two-sided platform model. These firms will compete on being the easiest to do business with and being able to drive significant value for the users, the product companies, and third-party customers. This is an attractive landscape but the most difficult model to fully build out. Most firms will transition through one of the previous three options before fully committing to option 4.

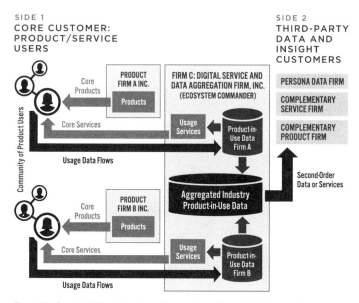

Figure 20 – Service Platform Experience Aggregator and Ecosystem Commander.

REACHING TO BE AN ECOSYSTEM COMMANDER

As the Connected World forms, a class of firms will emerge that could dominate a large part of the value chain. These Ecosystem Commanders will be a relatively small number of firms with considerable influence on how the connecting world evolves.

We choose to reuse the term "commanders" as a reference to terminology once used in legacy product and service industries. In the past, certain firms were designated as "channel commanders." This term referred to a single intermediary within a supply chain that became so dominant within the channel that it could dictate advantageous terms of business to the remainder of the supply chain channel both upstream to the producers of products or services and downstream toward the actual purchasers or consumers. Walmart is an example of a channel commander from the pre-e-commerce era. Through its consumer loyalty, the company yields influence over the OEMs of the products sold at Walmart stores, usually at the expense of OEM profit and to the benefit of the retail chain. Amazon is an example of an internet retail channel commander that has used many of the same general principles of growing a large community of frequent shoppers. What is common with both Walmart and Amazon in creating the commander role model is the relationship with the actual shopper or customer and the intention to grow aggressively.

In the connecting world, digital service firms that play the role of data aggregators, such as the one in figure 20, have the potential to emerge as Ecosystem Commanders. If firm C is able to attract a critical mass of firms into utilizing its core aggregating service offering, then it begins building the very ingredient required to become a Commander, which is customer usage data. If firm C is able to effectively create a portfolio of compelling services based on usage offered across multiple product or service firms, it can take over ownership of the customer's experience from the product OEM or service providers. At this point, customers could change product suppliers but keep the same usage data services. In fact, it's the continuity of the data services, irrespective of the manufacturer of the product, that dramatically weakens a product company's ability to create repeat purchase loyalty. In a Connected World, where the services offered by an Ecosystem Commander become more relevant to consumers than the actual product itself, the product has been commoditized.

In today's connecting world, Google, Amazon, Apple, Samsung, and Microsoft each have sufficient access to people and their behavior patterns that they may be able to leverage this to create broad ecosystems in which they play the dominant role. These data-centric companies are positioned to cross between traditional industries on the back of customer information. This can already be seen. Both Google and Apple dominate in the space of personal computing devices. They have also reached into the smart home and personal entertainment space and are now working on the connected car, considering mobility services. Amazon has acquired a major grocery chain and is venturing into the medical supply and pharmaceutical distribution services. These firms aren't simply personal electronics or personal computing companies. They are cross-industry giants with significant influence over the expectations that many people (i.e., users, customers) have of how seamless an experience should be in and across industry boundaries, which, as we've discussed, are crucial for relevancy in the Connected World. These emerging Ecosystem Commanders have become significant players in both sides of the two-sided platform business model.

Today's companies would be well advised to dedicate time and consideration to understanding the potential of participating within an ecosystem and the accompanying risks and rewards as they prepare for the Connected World. A few firms will rise to the level of being Ecosystem Commanders in the Connected World, managing the flow of data and usage experience across multiple ecosystems of connected industries. As such, they will take on a kind of oligopoly power over the ecosystem and create competition among product companies in order to participate both in the ecosystem as well as with the product end users.

BUILDING A BETTER MOUSETRAP: A BUSINESS STRATEGY STORY

The old adage, "Build a better mousetrap," does actually occur. There are still the old spring-loaded wooden traps that snap mechanically to kill the mouse. There are others with one-way doors that look more like metal cages with holes in them. Finally, there are some molded plastic traps that look similar to the metal caged version but have electronics embedded in them, like small circuit boards with room for Wi-Fi or cellular cards.

All three of them serve a similar purpose. They all remove mice from the local environment. They were also all inventions at one time, with each one possessing an innovative value. The first kills but only a single mouse, and once triggered it's unable to catch more mice until it's cleaned and reset. The second can capture multiple live mice, which makes it more efficient and possibly more humane. The third mousetrap can capture multiple mice, and the SIM card alerts the operator of the trap every time a mouse is caught, turning it into a connected mousetrap.

This simple technological advancement of the third trap affects the mousetrap's producer. At minimum, it requires different capabilities to produce the trap, which has implications for the firm's functional strategy. It can also present opportunities to shift the firm's business and corporate strategies. Perhaps they'll now offer monitoring services. Maybe their business is no longer selling traps. Now what they offer is a rodent-prevention service guarantee. These are options in the Connected World that weren't possible in a predigital landscape.

Connected mousetraps actually came on the market in the mid-2000s with the manufacturer offering them as a feature-rich addition to the standard model. The manufacturers, however, did not offer a rodent-prevention service. Rather, they offered the traps as connected products to customers, who then could create their own service offering. One of the business-to-business customers in the United Kingdom used the connected mousetrap to completely change its own business-level strategy with a new service offering. The firm was a property management company whose business was maintaining large commercial properties left vacant between leases. It guaranteed lease readiness. Until the advent of connected technologies, the company required hundreds of workers to patrol properties, keeping them secure and free of rodents.

A decade earlier, connected technologies came into the security space, which impacted the property management company. Cameras and sensors on doors and windows meant twenty-four-hour security guards were no longer needed. The company could remotely monitor the properties and send out a guard whenever it detected a possible breach of the perimeter. Even though it was able to reduce costs in security monitoring, the company still required a sizable force to walk the properties, check the traps, and put in replacement bait. When a trap snagged a mouse or a rodent, the company had three days to clear the dead animal before the smell became embedded into the structure of the facility. The cost of abating the smell outweighed the cost of having a human come and check on the trap once every three days, so a sizable human labor force was required.

The deployment of the connected traps reshaped the company. Even if the corporate strategy stayed the same, the business strategy now shifted. The owners recapitalized their company and purchased thousands of connected traps. They laid off two-thirds of their workforce, because they didn't need as many workers making the rounds. Now a small group of employees sit around a table in the pub and wait for their iPhones to buzz with an alert of a caught rodent. The workers then draw straws to see who's going to put down the pint and clean out the trap. The owners of the properties were unaware of the connected service capability, but the property management company was able to improve the quality of the service and lower the cost to deliver. This high margin could be used to underbid competition and take a larger market share. A true differentiated business strategy.

CONSIDERATIONS FOR A BUSINESS STRATEGY IN THE CONNECTING WORLD

The largest changes to the way firms will compete in the Connected World will be at the corporate strategy level and, more specifically, in the consideration of various new business model options. This isn't to imply that it's only at the corporate strategy layer where the Connected World creates potential for strategic change. The mousetrap scenario is an example of how the property management firm leveraged connected products to enhance its business strategy and offer a higher quality of service at a lower cost.

As connected technologies advance, opportunities for brand positioning and competitive differentiation with enhanced connected services increase. The seamlessness of the experience will emerge as one of the key business strategies in the connecting world. Look to some of the hospitality companies that are now allowing customers to use their phones as their room keys. Like modern airline travel, one can check in twenty-four hours in advance and take possession of the room's "key." This means no stop at the front desk, and heading directly to your room upon arrival, with the door simply unlocking as you approach. That is seamless. This single feature will likely be extended to handling other issues related to before, during, and after the stay. Building a more robust profile of preferences and PiU data of how the person uses the property can turn a generic hotel room into something highly personalized and make the guest feel as if he or she is sleeping in his or her own room. These technologies have started with hospitality firms that position themselves as premium, but the technologies will diffuse downward until they become ubiquitous within the hospitality industry. The connected features within all existing products and services will continue a march toward seamless integration of life experiences with minimal human intervention.

Firms still must be aware and aligned to what competitors are doing to enhance their service offerings and respond accordingly within their own business strategy.

The levers of the business strategy will remain more or less the same, dealing with product positioning, pricing, communication, and distribution. Still, the differentiation opportunities with these levers will expand through the continuous extension of connected services. The addition of services informed by PiU data must be done in a manner that appears logical within the positioning of the brand experience. The purchasers of a premium-priced, full-featured product would seemingly expect a matching core connected service offering. This is a basic consideration. Extensions of this matching must be considered when firms evaluate connecting the data flow of their customers with another complementary product or service.

Prior to the emergence of the Connected World, companies from time to time engaged in affinity marketing where two companies would agree to represent each other's brand on their products. The logic behind affinity marketing is that customers who bought one brand might be similar in profile to the customers who bought the other brand. For example, Ford Motor Company created a Harley-Davidson promotional package for its F-150 truck, offering it for more than a decade until ending it in 2012. In the Connected World, where products might integrate with services in the next step of a person's day, the choices a firm makes in selecting partners become important. Think back to our introduction, where our CEO's fork meshed with his health record, personal schedule, and transportation service. Such cross-industry connections will drive a relevant and seamless experience that extends far beyond the simple affinity marketing from the preconnected era. The seamless experience needs to not only transfer information but also needs to extend a similar level of experience.

During the time of transition, what we call the connecting world period, companies are feeling their way into an emerging ecosystem of interdependencies among firms. This is happening seamlessly in real time, and therefore the concept of product and service positioning differentiation becomes more nuanced. A firm that is attempting to offer the most basic product with limited features as part of a low-price strategy would seem to be miscast if it was integrating with complementary products or services that were positioning their products as high quality and full featured for premium prices. A crucial business strategy issue will be maintaining control over the choice among the inter- and intrabrand relationships. In the world of connected ecosystems, the choices firms make about positioning will have to be aligned with the ecosystem at large.

This interdependency within ecosystems also has an implication for how products and services will establish prices and, maybe more importantly, trade the value of user information. Consumers will expect consistency in pricing strategies relative to similar products and services within a seamless ecosystem. If some services are offered for free while others are charging, yet both are gaining access to user information, ecosystem conflict may occur. Connected ecosystems may move to adopt revenue collection models that consolidate a number of services toward a single collection point. In such a model, the price of a consolidated basket of services from multiple connected firms will be set based on criteria that reflect the general positioning of the entire basket of services. One of the most basic issues for ecosystems to resolve is whether users will pay a single billing agent representing the ecosystem or pay multiple participating companies within the ecosystem. In a single-payer model, the Ecosystem Commander must determine the service models offered. Will they offer subscription fees, charge only for usage, offer a trade of value for user information, or a combination of these options? These issues are far from being resolved, but they are clearly on the business strategy horizon, and your teams should be considering them.

It's time for you, the leader, to create the strategy for the firm. Existing business models' options and ecosystem realities, as well as internal constraints should inform this strategy. In the Connected World, as you can see in figure 21, a firm's business strategy will have to consider maintaining competitiveness along two dimensions. As the environment continues to demand more sophisticated integration models, the business model building block options that you choose will guide you to different strategies.

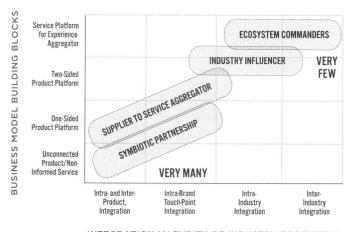

Figure 21 – Business Model to Integration Matrix.

There will be competition among ecosystems, each one seeking to position itself as offering some unique value to consumers. In today's world, a consumer purchasing a smartphone decides between the ecosystems of the Apple IOS and Google Android. Imagine needing to make the same type of choice when it comes to personal transportation, residential living, or recreational activities. It will no longer be sufficient for firms to differentiate themselves from other companies. They now need to be part of an ecosystem that has differentiated itself from other ecosystems. We can expect that the dominant product or service in the ecosystem, the eco-commander, will determine the basic attributes of differentiation, such as low cost or high quality. Other potential participants will either seek to align with the eco-commander or seek an alternative ecosystem in which to participate.

FUNCTIONAL STRATEGY IMPLICATIONS

If a company that made disposable diapers added sensors to its product to detect abnormal levels of hormones, bacteria, or viruses, and used the data to inform caretakers or the medical community for potential early diagnosis of disease, would it still be a diaper company? Does it still compete on the same basis (i.e., absorbency and softness)? Does the firm require different internal capabilities, and will different value chain partners be required to live these new corporate and business strategies? Do the existing capabilities within the IT department require some adaptation? If that same firm decided that the actual diaper production was something that they could outsource to a former competitor, would the firm need to retain the internal capabilities related to diaper production at all?

Welcome to the underworld of functional strategy, the place where brilliance in corporate and business strategies will shine in the market or not. Whereas corporate and business strategies are formulations, functional strategy is about delivery implementation. The output of the functional strategy is the portfolio of internal and some controlled external capabilities necessary to deliver the output of the organization. Corporate and business strategy domains are intentions with respect to the external environment. The functional strategy is internally focused, operational delivery.

To create the correct impression of the importance of the functional strategy to the success of the firm, let's follow some simple logic. In order for a firm to compete in the Connected World, it may change its business model and aspire to compete differently. In order to deliver on this change, the firm will need to adapt its internal capabilities. It's likely it will have to add capabilities, enhance some existing capabilities, and potentially discontinue some other capabilities altogether. The difference between a firm's current profile of capabilities and the profile of capabilities necessary to compete in the Connected World is the firm's capability gap. As shown in figure 22, the functional strategy layer links step 1 and step 2 of the First Mile. This capability gap isn't only to reflect the missing capabilities; it also includes the magnitude of all the changes necessary, including partially enhancing and even discontinuing some existing capabilities. Such changes require internal decisions to be made and an effort undertaken to transform the firm to deliver on the new intentions for the marketplace.

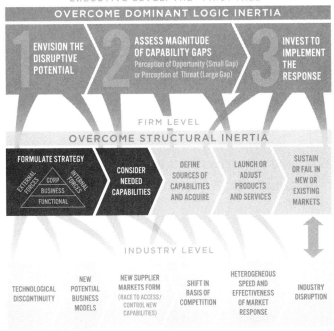

Figure 22 – CGS Connected World Transformation Framework—Strategy to Capability Linkage.

The magnitude of the capability gap defines the magnitude of the internal transformation necessary to realize the functional strategy of the firm. This simple logic is one of the fundamental premises of this book. The Connected World represents a significant shift in the basis of competition. Business models will be different, differentiation will be different, and therefore internal capabilities must be different. Consequently, all firms must consider a potential internal transformation to their functional strategy in order to compete in the Connected World. The faster executives realize there is a race that has already started to acquire access to new capabilities, the greater the chance they will survive in the Connected World.

When we look at the corporate strategy, we can see that option 1, becoming a B2B supplier, allows for many firms to keep doing what they're already doing. The biggest shift isn't focused on changing capabilities but rather a large transformation in culture, especially if the current firm faces directly to a market consumer and in the connecting world they become a B2B provider. All other corporate strategy and business strategy choices will require a shift, depending on the origins of the company. The magnitude of the functional strategy change is directly proportionate to the magnitude of the corporate and business strategy changes. Hence, it's imperative for organizations to become clear on their corporate and business strategies for the Connected World before they begin determining the impact on their functional strategy. The intention in the marketplace should drive the delivery mechanisms. To do it in reverse and adjust the internal structure without an explicit external purpose is naive.

The goal of getting the functional strategy right is crucial, and its importance is reflected in the way it dominates the middle row of our Connected World Transformation framework. We will focus on it in the next chapter. Fortunately, functional strategy changes are something most senior executives can get comfortable with. It happens frequently, and some portion of your leadership team has been part of one during their career. The difference this time may be the specific capabilities in focus and being driven by industry disruption, corporate and business strategy shifts, and the ideas of a top leader who believes your firm must move quickly because of an incredible opportunity or terrifying threat.

THE RIGHT APPROACH

We can't predict what the correct corporate, business, and functional strategies will be for any particular firm. We do, however, with high confidence, advise clients on what we believe to be the right approach, which is reconsidering the potential for changes in corporate and business strategies and then determining the impact of such choices on the functional strategy. In order to be fast in running the First Mile, the process must run from top down, but the capability gap should be assessed from today's current capability profile up. If the gap is considered to be too large for the firm to close, given the availability of capital to invest, then the process must run in the opposite direction, with leaders determining what reductions in scope of the business and corporate strategy would be necessary based on the capabilities that can be acquired. Firms can decide to stay with their current strengths or decide to reinvent themselves by aggressively seeking to acquire new capabilities in order to launch a new business model. The challenge is the uncertainty of undertaking these strategy reviews at multiple levels within your firm, when it's not clear what your competitors may be doing at the same time. Start the preparation now.

Now is a good time to call out a couple of truisms we find ourselves repeating to leaders facing these transformations. "Features don't make a future." Many leaders in companies stepping into the Connected World focus on launching a simple connected feature and then celebrate. We are advocates of simple features and minimum viable products to help get firms moving in the right direction. Celebrating with the team over early and small successes should also be applauded. Nevertheless, the responsibility needs to stay with the executives. You must realize that these early features are just the beginning of your connected journey. If you make minimal investment in capabilities and celebrate the feature as if you were truly preparing, then you're probably suffering from the willful blindness we discussed earlier. Don't let a connected feature on a product strategy road map convince you that you're preparing to compete in the connecting world. Your responsibility runs deeper than that.

"Make a platform not a product." We have spent a lot of time in this chapter talking about the importance of taking part in an ecosystem with a two-sided platform. If your product isn't able to support large and diverse users, or if third parties won't be able to leverage it, then you're likely on your way toward a commodity role as a supplier. The next time you attend a product review meeting, ask the team if they're considering new users in the future, and how easily an entirely different user group can leverage this product in the future. What makes a hotel room not a teaching environment or an outpatient medical facility? If a cell phone can be a camera, computer, gaming console, weather station, and phone, why can't your product do a few more things?

You may have a lot to consider for your firm's strategy, but you're not alone. Look at century-old industries, and it's not surprising that many of them are starting to make drastic moves. Whether it's media, retail, or auto, industries are attempting to be proactive. Take the retail industry, for example. It isn't surprising that the leaders are proactive start-ups with new business models preparing for the Connected World. Disruptive forces such as Amazon, Shipt, and Cargo have been moving the technology forward every day for years. Everyone inside the industry can feel the outside pressure and knows that it is not waiting for them.

This is the moment for you, the reader, to push pause for a moment and ask if your particular firm is ready. If the answer is no, then you need to think about why. If it's because you can't see it at all, then maybe you should solicit some other opinions. If you think the answer is no because you believe the technology around you isn't ready, then take a look at other industries and ask yourself again. It's coming fast. So what can you do today in terms of strategy to ready for the change? Put statements down that change your value system to align to the Connected World and think about how these new values will force you to shift your strategy. Then return to the book and read the final chapters so you can begin the work of acquiring the capabilities needed to compete.

CHAPTER

6

FORGE NEW CAPABILITIES

"What's your special sauce for the Connected World?"

McDonald's always referenced its "special sauce," which is what differentiated its Big Mac from the competition's burgers. The real special sauce for McDonald's wasn't actually what was on the burger but more about how it consistently reproduced its experience, consistently managed its global franchises, and controlled some of the most sought-after real estate in the United States. All of McDonald's competitors had a way to make their burgers, manage experiences, and find locations, and they each had similar functions needed for a "fast food" eatery. What they didn't have was McDonald's unique execution. They didn't have the right capability.

The activities of a company are rarely secrets. Often, they

are blatantly obvious when being performed. Sometimes they are so obvious that the organization is shaped around them, and a sign is hung in the hallway, or a title is placed on a business card calling it out for everyone to see: Marketing, Engineering, Sales. Capabilities, on the other hand, are more difficult to recognize. They are the bundles of critical expertise, technology, and skills that form the basis of current or future business success.

While the business strategy is a statement of external intent to differentiate relative to other competitors, the capabilities are the internal means of delivering on that intent. Although all companies in an industry share a relatively common set of business functions, companies do differ on their degree of proficiency in terms of how they execute them. Some of that differentiation is relevant to how the company competes. So business strategy and capability to deliver on strategy are in fact two sides of the same coin.

Each enterprise must choose not only the functions necessary to compete in the business in which they choose—corporate strategy alignment—but also the unique and, hopefully, differentiating ways to compete in that business through their capabilities—business strategy alignment.

An easy and relevant example from a product company is

the "function" of manufacturing versus the "capability" of agile manufacturing. Every product firm must manufacture their product. Some will see this as core and create an internal manufacturing function, while others may outsource manufacturing to a supplier or contract manufacturing company. Many enterprises will create a department that will have the responsibility for this function. The organization's capability is not manufacturing but rather the way in which they achieve competitive advantage from this function. Agile manufacturing is an example of this differentiation. This capability gives the company the ability to rapidly pivot and react to market dynamics more quickly.

When capabilities are created deliberately, they are resourced appropriately with sufficient capital investment and operational support to ensure the differentiation outcome is not compromised. A key indicator of what the top executives perceive to be the key capabilities can be found in how internal budgets—both capital and operating—are distributed. Business functions receiving disproportionate budget resources are what executives feel to be the true capabilities of the company. An old adage is, "Follow the budget if you want to best understand how executives believe they will earn their bonuses."

In the Connected World, the differentiating capabilities may shift even further. Sticking with our example of the manufacturing function, for instance, the differentiating capabilities in the Connected World may even extend beyond the typical production facility. Over-the-air update (OTA) is emerging as an extension of the manufacturing function. It allows producers of internet-connected things to update their products while waiting to be sold, or even while being used by the customer post-sale. This is a specialized and differentiated capability that will help companies reduce cost, act faster, and be user focused.

All of this is much more complex than modeling a new function. It's about understanding what "special sauce" is needed to make your corporate recipe work.

THE NEXT LEG OF THE FIRST MILE

In previous chapters we discussed the First Mile of Transformation in the connecting world that will guide a firm's leadership in exploiting a technological discontinuity. We have discussed how leaders must *Envision the Disruptive Potential*. This requires seeing beyond the patterns of the dominant logic within the industry, envisioning a new basis of competition, and forming strategies to capitalize on the market and the firm's position in it. As seen in figure 23, the next step is to *Assess Magnitude of Capability Gaps* by pulling the cover off the company's strategies. It's about taking inventory of current capabilities and asking whether they're sufficient for the new strategy or, if not, how the firm will gain access to them. Only once this occurs can the executives begin ratifying the strategic changes and *Invest to Implement the Response.*

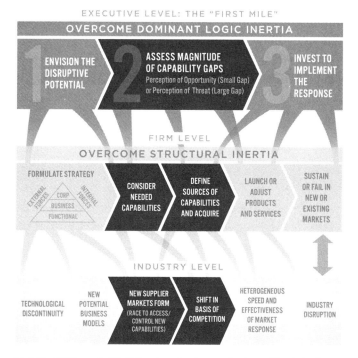

Figure 23 – CGS Connected World Transformation Framework – Assess Magnitude of Capability Gaps.

Ignoring the oncoming disruption and not fully appreciating its significance on the current strategy and capability balance are two common mistakes. The most frequent misstep, however, is assuming you can gather a few deputies in a room, decide you're going to change strategy, and feel like your work is done. Without understanding how to operationalize the strategy, it is dead in the water. If you don't set the tone of real change and then commit the necessary resources to rebalance the internal capabilities to fit the new strategies, not much happens other than some executive's rhetoric and a communications campaign that may be able to satisfy investors for a few quarters. Further, it's not about simply resourcing new capabilities. Some existing capabilities will continue to enable the new strategies and must continue to be resourced at potentially different levels. Other existing capabilities will constrain, or actually work against, the new strategies. These constraining capabilities must be dampened. In many cases, this means taking away resources or divesting of a function. One true measure of whether a company is truly engaged in a transformation process is the degree to which it has stopped resourcing once-critical legacy capabilities that are holding the company back. Let's look at the transformations of product and digital companies.

Product, or "things," companies are built on industrial economics, whereas digital companies are based on information economics and network effects, such as number of users or sensors (sources of information) in the ecosystem. A things firm interested in transitioning to compete in the Connected World will look at the world of information economics and network effects and see new paths to revenue. The dilemma is simple: how does it get to the new paths without sacrificing the capabilities that allow it to build great products? Even if it determines to keep existing capabilities that differentiate the way it manufactures, designs, distributes, or services, it will still be forced to come up with a slightly different recipe for the special sauce known as differentiation, taking ingredients from information economic models and network effects. The connecting world will require it add new capabilities, such as moving data, and storing, analyzing, applying, and eventually monetizing it.

Many of the base *functions* necessary in the Connected World may appear to already exist inside of a things company's internal IT department. Unfortunately, the name of the department doesn't necessarily mean it's a great fit to build these new market-facing capabilities. Chief information officers may very well be the right people to lead a portion of the transformation toward becoming a connect company, but they will need to be given many more resources and span of control than those they are typically entrusted with in the inward-facing IT department of product companies. This legacy department isn't a group with an outside market-looking view—a problem because most of the changes being discussed are customer or market facing. This leaves the things companies with the option to build the capability, buy it, or look for partnerships to enable the functional strategy.

A digital company, one accustomed to creating, maintaining, and applying software and data, will have a completely different transformation path. It already knows how to collect revenue from subscriptions, services-based fees, or the second side of a two-sided business model. It's the idea of building a thing, or hard product, that is somewhat out of leftfield for many digital companies. If a company like Google wants to build a car, for example, it already has a way to create the software and a marketplace to sell the services that could be rendered inside of the car. What it doesn't have is the car, or a sense of how to properly plan for long production cycles and large capital investments with long pay-off cycles required for vehicle manufacturing. It will force them to think through a whole new set of capabilities built on industrial economics. It will learn either on its own or through a partnership how to invest large sums of capital to create a manufacturing line with the high-quality standards needed to build complex products that can't be updated with a simple push of a button.

At a macrolevel, the shifts for things and digital firms are almost mirror opposites of each other and easy to break down. Things firms have the capabilities tied to the "T" side of IoT and are grounded in the world of industrial economics. Digital firms have the "I" capabilities fairly tuned up, are tied to the information economics, and are comfortable with the network effect. Now these companies will need to find ways to acquire the opposite set. Legacy firms will need to grow capabilities focused on binding these two worlds together.

Once leaders understand their firm's capability gap, they can come up with a plan for how to create or transform the enabling capabilities while phasing out the constraining ones. There's a frightening tendency of top executives to underestimate the persistence of the existing structure. People come to work every day expecting to do more or less what they did the day before. Even if they read about the organization's major transformation plans in the monthly newsletter, they're still inclined to continue doing their jobs until specifically told otherwise. This inertia is true whether the person is a vice-president or an administrative assistant. You can't rely on an organic process to dampen the constraining capabilities. It needs to be explicitly clear to workers that this might be what you did yesterday, but *this* is what is now expected from this point forward. Because of the tremendous pushback you can expect, it will be prudent in certain cases to put the enabling capabilities in a protected structure, such as a special team, a new division, or a wholly separate company. We generally believe that centralization of the new protected capability is the most efficient way to launch and protect. This will give those responsible for it room and time to incubate. You'll not only need to protect these new and enhanced capabilities, but you'll also have to defend them until the transformation becomes part of the culture and new corporate structure.

So on which capabilities do you need to focus? Well, every

firm is different. This means it's impossible to tell you which capabilities for your firm will be new, transformed, or suppressed. A new capability for one company could be transformed for another, and a capability in need of enhancement for one firm may be the one that's constraining for a different company. What should be clear is that each transforming firm will have new, transforming, and suppressed capabilities as it learns to compete in the connecting world.

NURTURING NEW CAPABILITIES

The first group of capabilities to consider is the ones that are going to be net new for your firm. When looking at your capability gap analysis, these should stand out as outliers to your current business. They are skills you never would've considered in the past and likely ones buried deep in the organization. You may struggle to understand the skills needed or whom on your executive team you should even use as your counsel on the matter. If you can step back far enough and look at your firm with fresh and honest eyes, you'll be able to see whether your firm currently possesses the capability. New, in other words, is something you'll recognize when you *don't* see it. The team helping you analyze the gap will need to be realistic as well. If an intern is the extent of the investment you have made in a capability set that you now clearly see as part of the future of the company, this is not transforming an established function. After all, what will happen in the fall when she heads back to school? It needs to be treated like a new launch.

A few years ago, a proud junior executive, whom we will leave nameless to protect the innocent, explained to us that because they had a "provisioning" capability in their IT department, they were basically ready to roll out their connected product. When we dug into this claim, we discovered that the large product company had a part-time student who provisioned—set up devices and registered them on the cellular network—new smartphones for the company's executives. Yes, they had a process and simple system (Microsoft Excel spreadsheet and a web page provided by the cellular carrier). Yes, they had a person, a physical work environment, and even an emerging culture, one could argue. They had all this for under one hundred executives who were authorized to carry mobile devices. In the first year, they were planning to launch between thirty and seventy thousand connected devices to market through retailers. They didn't have the provisioning capability necessary. Not even close. They had a gap, and eventually their executives realized they needed a new capability around market-based provisioning to ensure their products were connected and functioning so they could support all the use cases they imagined. They partnered with a third party specializing in complex product provisioning and had a successful launch to market.

As you consider adding capabilities, you'll be forced to consider the nuances of how you make these investments. This is a time to widen your perspective and challenge your perception of what's important to a business moving forward. Say you're a digital services company considering turning out a connected product. You recognize the need for a net new function of manufacturing. You have options, one of which is to mirror those companies with hundreds of years of manufacturing experience and grow it internally and with a proven approach. Another possibility is to outsource those pieces to experts in the field. A third, more innovative but less proven option is to partner on traditional manufacturing but place a larger bet on an emerging capability, such as 3-D/4-D printing, or additive manufacturing.

It starts with recognizing the gap. The next challenge is understanding and deciding on your options of how to fill it. Does a proven approach lower the investment's risk? Or is it an approach whose efficacy was proven in the Unconnected World and would actually lock you into yesterday's market dynamics? Finally, you will need to determine what capabilities you want to bring inside your organization that will enable the differentiating you seek, and which do you simply need in order to gain access to a supplier or partnership arrangement.

WHAT'S OLD IS NEW AGAIN: TRANSFORMING CAPABILITIES

Transformation of current capabilities will come in several flavors. Some capabilities simply need to be scaled—doing more, the same way your firm currently does it. We will call these elevated capabilities. They will need to be elevated in prominence, and likely will draw more expenses, but not require a tremendous level of investment in how to scale them. Other capabilities will need to significantly change, not necessarily in scale, but in how they are positioned and performed. We will call these converted capabilities.

Let's first discuss elevated capabilities. Many companies today already have capabilities critical to compete in the Connected World. The reality of the digital age has forced things companies to manage, analyze, and exploit information, and consider issues such as how to store and process big data. Some companies may even have a team devoted to discovering insights from this data through analytics. More and more, we see companies dip their toes into the IoT water and begin collecting information through sensor integration. These digital capabilities are seeping into all types of businesses, although they'll likely need tuning and scaling for the connecting world. You'll have to invest heavily in elevating these current, relevant capabilities. Right now, teams with names such as Big Data Analytics, Information Security, Predictive Analytics, and AI may seem to be "nice to have" or part of an emerging technologies group, but to prepare for the Connected World, you'll need to begin emphasizing them.

Many service companies have pet "thing" projects born out of R&D efforts or in innovation groups. Look at some of the insurance companies that are experimenting with drones for inspection purposes. Perhaps the simple products were contract manufactured to allow for faster ramp-up timing, or purchased and then "hacked" for a specific use. Whether it's designing, manufacturing, or "hacking," chances are that some of the "T" capabilities have been incubating in the "I" organization.

It's possible that many of the capabilities you need are buried inside your organization, although they are stuck in an unlikely department such as internal IT or the customer call center, areas where technology was treated more like a necessary evil instead of a strategic differentiator. Sometimes they are even mature and just need to be scaled. Regardless of the history, legacy firms will need to elevate these capabilities to fit their connected strategies.

Then there are the converted capabilities that will require true transformation. There are situations where a function already exists, but how it is executed will need to be altered. In other words, the capability "special sauce" will need to use a new recipe.

These converted capability transformations are going to make a huge part of your connected strategic plan. They form the core of the functional strategy mentioned in the last chapter. Capabilities that need changing are hidden all over the organization. Once you start shifting the corporate and business strategies, you will have no choice but to address the functional layer. Consider a few of the following that your firm likely already possesses, regardless if you are a product or services company.

Almost every commercial company sells things and collects payments. They may call this the order-to-cash capability. How ready is your order-to-cash capability to assist your company to compete in the connecting world? Will it need to be transformed? Right now, your accounts receivable may be set up for only one-time sales. How flexible is it for a business strategy involving the sale of services on the back of your product? It's a transformed capability in the sense that your company won't survive without it. It may not require hiring a PhD from the top engineering school, but you won't collect money aligned to the new business strategy if it's not transformed. This sort of transformation is often missed as new connectivity is explored, but it will be critical on day one of operations.

Or take marketing. Almost every company has had a marketing capability since day one of operations, but unless they were an internet-based software company, they've probably never had a direct communication line open with the end consumer. Surely, they've never had the ability to be in constant communication with the end customer every time the product or service is in use. Real-time feedback, however, is now a reality. The marketing function, therefore, will have to transform for the Connected World, too. Product-in-use (PiU) data coupled with OTA updates allow for an entirely different kind of relationship with your customers. Marketing will have to bring together the unique and individual nature of a mature CRM capability and a progressive and always-on marketing capability. The product can fundamentally change as it connects. If you're interested in driving loyalty, then what better place to market to your current customers than at the point of experience? Furthermore, for adding new customers, why not use the "fleet" of your products already in the market? If a consumer sees a product they're interested in, they no longer have to visit a store to learn about it. Now they can learn everything about it on the internet. Many products themselves can "talk" to potential consumers in nonretail settings. A car parked on the street can broadcast to consumers walking past, helping them consider specific information such as special features. They can even schedule a real-time test drive. The product itself can be the greatest tool to ensure consistent brand ambassadorship. If done right, connected products can become a true marketing touchpoint and shorten the cycle from awareness to sale.

One of the most logical conversions will be linked to security. Most companies, through their audit function or IT department, already have a position called chief information security officer (CISO). As connected products emerge, the capabilities around connected digital security need to elevate. A hack that denies access to a server used to take down a website. It can now take down an entire manufacturing facility, smart home, or a connected vehicle traveling at seventy miles per hour. Cyber physical security, therefore, is one of the top elevated capabilities in a connected company.

Not everything needs to change, but nearly everything likely will. Even accounting will face pressure to transform. Right now, you abide by some basic accounting rules and file reports about what you have and whether it's depreciated in value. The entire accounting process is predicated on the value of physical goods and their capital value. In the future, information will be the new currency. The capability to exploit information will drive value. Is the accounting function prepared for a future where you'll have to report the value of data to shareholders and auditors?

This isn't an exhaustive list. It's also not a science. It's essentially a way for one to rank capabilities by degrees of importance. If a capability is critical to the strategy, it will be in focus, and investing resources is crucial. You probably want to host it in-house or acquire it through a strong partnership. The transformation is really all about finding your road to the right capabilities. Taking inventory is a critical first step, followed by determining whether you need to acquire, elevate, or convert them.

MAKE ROOM BY SUPPRESSING CERTAIN CAPABILITIES

There's no checklist of the capabilities you'll need to survive the Connected World. It's about understanding the need to operate differently from how you did in the past. There will be large players in the industry who want to get their hands on every possible capability in order to leave their options open. Smaller companies will have no choice but to become specialists in certain areas and strike partnerships to fulfill the other capabilities. The decision mostly comes down to your organization's current control over existing channels, how difficult it will be for your organization to respond, and the deepness of your pockets. If you are an agile organization with lots of money and control over the channels, then you'll probably want to try and control as much of the value chain as possible. You can afford to keep your old capabilities. Smaller firms must be realistic about how they can best get to the other side in one piece. It's about moving the needle of the right capabilities fast enough to stay relevant in the Connected World conversation.

Resources are finite, and this fact will cause considerable

angst for you as the transition launches. Capabilities will compete with other capabilities for the organization's scarce resources, and you'll decide which projects to fund. Will you invest all of your resources into building these new capabilities for the Connected World, or will you hold back somewhat so you can continue to support the capabilities driving your current business as you go through the transition? For some time, you will have to do both, but to what extent and at what cost to the new strategy?

As you decide the pace of change, some capabilities will likely be seen more as overlap as opposed to gaps. These capabilities, which no longer need to be differentiated in the connecting world, are the easiest to suppress or eliminate to free up resources. This is similar to the mousetrap example from the last chapter where the need for personnel to walk the properties declined when sensors were attached. Likewise, capabilities in your company will also become commoditized. The function may need to remain, but the way it is performed will shift. There are plenty of examples in the connecting world from drivers to receptionists. For instance, goods will still need to be moved, but they may be done autonomously. If you don't believe in the picture we're painting, visit an Amazon warehouse where no humans are allowed on 90 percent of the floor—namely, the areas where robots move the goods to sorting stations and trucks. What will be your function that is commoditized? What capabilities were differentiated in the Unconnected World that will no longer be needed?

IN-FOCUS CAPABILITIES FOR THE CONNECTING WORLD

As previously mentioned, there is no master list of the right capabilities to add, abandon, or transform first. This is what makes open market competition interesting. The winning equation is different for every firm and leader. Like many topics in this book, however, there are some observable patterns. In this case, there are capabilities that routinely demand more attention from leaders determining how to fill capability gaps. We list a handful of them here:

CAPABILITY	DESCRIPTION	FIRM TYPE MOST TRANSFORMED
Over-the-Air (OTA) Configuration and Software Updates	Making a product able to send and receive data allows for remote configuration and post-sale customization and new features monetization. The product can provide PiU information, and the company can service remotely as well as sell new configurations and features.	Product
Configuration Management	With the likelihood of OTA updates, a deep capability of managing many configurations of products in market will proliferate and will need to be accessible by technical and customer service personnel consistently.	Product
Third-Party Services Management (Side 2 of the Platform)	As the connected things and environments provide PiU information from the user customers (side 1), companies will need skills to create and manage services created from PiU data to provide to the side 2 customers, and the ability to offer services from side 2 companies to side 1 communities.	Both
Ecosystem Management (e.g., API Management)	Establishing a strong brand presence and commercial contracts within an ecosystem of companies to provide end users of ecosystem products and services that fit well with others in the ecosystem.	Both

CAPABILITY	DESCRIPTION	FIRM TYPE MOST TRANSFORMED
Big Data and Data Science (Analytics, Machine Learning)	All of the new information and perceived value that comes with it will demand a broad array of capabilities linked to how to move, store, analyze, predict, and secure information that comes from sensors, products, and environments.	Both
Change/ Transformation Management	A cross-functional group that manages every aspect of the change from the product/service itself to how it's marketed. Many firms already have people managing either the product or the information side, but not both (e.g., a manufacturing line is typically updated only every few years, while digital products have software that is updated almost every night).	Both
Advanced CRM and Customization	PiU-informed CRM, and managing customization profiles in the cloud.	Both
Enterprise Innovation Management (Hackathons)	Digital technology moves at a rate that can be dizzying for organizations. If your company wants to survive past this current transformation, it will need the capability to keep up with the constant advancement of technology.	Both
Artificial Intelligence Management (e.g., Bots, AI)	This is a forming capability from building and supporting self-learning algorithms to managing teams with members that are AI engines. There is significant change embodied in this capability area.	Both
Cross-Platform User-Experience (UX) Design, Personalization, and Rationalization	With developing ecosystems, it's imperative to start thinking about how your user experience meshes with the experiences of other products and services. It requires a broader approach to design. UX/user interface (UI), therefore, is another capability companies will usually elevate.	Both
Cyber Physical Security	As digital technology permeates traditional products and information flows from environment to environment, security will become a much sought-after capability. Locking the filing cabinet, the data center, or the gates will no longer be enough.	Both
Advanced and Agile Manufacturing (e.g., 3-D/4-D Printing)	Companies that have manufactured things for years have learned how to make physical goods with a level of quality for an appropriate price. Digital firms don't have the same discipline due to the low cost of reconfiguring and updating software. As physical products become platforms, the lessons from both legacy spaces will need to mesh.	Digital
Crowdsourced Design and Build (e.g., Maker Movement, Gamification)	For traditional firms that have always conceived, designed, engineered, and produced their products and services inside their controlled supply chain, the advent of leaning on the actual users to do more than use will be a massive change. "Crowd" management, training, and encouragement constitute an emerging art to keep users engaged and costs low.	Both

This is not *the* list, but it proves to be an interesting starter for executives having a hard time understanding how the new environment or corporate and business strategies will impact operations. Add this simple list to one with almost fifty percent of traditional functions in your company and you'll likely have the list you need. An analysis we recently performed for a product industry revealed that more than two-thirds of their market-facing capabilities and half of their nonmarket-facing functions will be impacted. The change doesn't happen all at once, but few will not be effective in one way, shape, or form. Competing in the connecting world is different, and that is the point.

A CAPABILITY THAT MAY RISE ABOVE THE REST

A firm's corporate strategy department may guide the choices regarding which capabilities are most critical to the future operations, but it's not always enough to lead your company to the Promised Land. The ability to form complex and nontraditional cross-enterprise partnerships may be the hidden capability to truly unlock the potential of your future firm. Loosely labeled Partnership Management, this capability will be forced to find meaningful connections between entities that may have never had a reason to communicate in the past.

As the world connects, new ecosystems will form to help bring informed experiences to customers. This means product experiences may inform one another by passing information, even though the products themselves will never be operated together. PiU data from a mobility product may inform a smart home product. A personal scheduling service may inform a food distribution service. A product used at work may inform a personal health-care product. Each of these connected products will require at minimum two companies to form some kind of relationship. They'll need to envision, design, and build the experience and the technical transfer of information. They'll also need to negotiate the principles of this cooperation, the rules of information transfer and ownership, and the commercial value for such a relationship.

Currently, firms may have some partnerships. The strategy group, the business development group, or the purchasing department may have been involved in negotiating these one-off alliances, which is fine because they're probably minor partnerships. The ones driving your connected experience will be core to your business. Partnerships will require constant monitoring, adjustment, and potentially, renegotiations.

Partnership management is crucial for firms that cannot own the entire connected value chain. As you begin connecting your product, or using PiU data to inform your service, you'll have to consider the customers, who will want your connected experience only if it seamlessly integrates with other products and services in the ecosystem.

Partnership Management is a relatively small investment, but it can mean a world of difference for companies as they enter the Connected World. Large firms that are flush with cash may be able choose not to partner, as they can diversify and buy nontraditional experiences to integrate. A majority of firms in the world aren't in this position, which means they'll have to find a role in these expanded ecosystems that have emerged from more traditional value chains.

Don't wait to find your partnership managers. The capability may be the critical building block on the road to becoming an Ecosystem Commander. Suppose you clearly see the market is changing and come up with a brilliant strategy. Sadly, you lack the partnership management capability, so a turf war breaks out when you hand it off to your implementation team. The purchasing team, who are measured on cost savings, are trying to grind down the price point, and the process comes to a stop. In the meantime, your natural partners have formed a relationship with a different company. When your company finally gets its act together, everyone is already paired up and on the dance floor. No one looks cool dancing alone, so invest quickly in building collaborative capabilities, and focus on finding partners to grow and learn with.

THE RACE OF YOUR LIFE

Filling the gaps in capabilities between how you compete today and how you'll compete in the Connected World is the key to implementing your strategy. We discussed in previous chapters the strategic choices that the firm's leadership needs to make. What business will the firm be in? What way will it compete in this new connected business? And as discussed earlier in this chapter, which capabilities are most required? Once these three decisions have been set, it's time to implement the strategy.

All too often, during a technological discontinuity, the excitement of the technology, the massive industry disruption, or the firm's strategic options overshadow the implementation phase. This, however, is where the "rubber meets the road." It's where we've made a career of driving real successful change, and it's where you will make or break the success of your firm and likely this phase of your career. In the broadest sense, strategy implementation is all about obtaining and exploiting the right capabilities. Timing is imperative. If you wait too long, the capabilities may no longer be available to buy, and your firm may not have the time or money to develop them internally. Transition too quickly, and you may beat the market but suffer lack of traction while the market catches up.

Adding, transforming, and suspending capabilities will

be the greatest determinant of your firm's success. You must minimally match the adoption speed of your future industry and access and control the supply of scarce new capabilities before your competitors do. The complicating factor is that because all industries are facing the effects of the connecting world at generally the same time, some of these capabilities are not only being sought after by your recognized competitors but also those in adjacent industries. It's a compounding problem that is often talked about through phrases such as "talent gap." Call it what you want; it's a race for survival that has many runners looking to identify and capture the same critical skills and capabilities.

A major factor in executing these changes is the speed at which you're able to dampen the internal conflicts and inertia created by honoring the old structure versus clearly driving toward the new one that you're trying to build for the Connected World. Once your leadership team is able to drive through this noise, the company can see the disruption and adjust the capabilities. A failure to reconcile the clash will constrain the speed at which you get to where you're trying to go, and speed, as we've argued before, is what matters most.

The not-so-simple decision that you and your colleagues need to make is how you will gain access to these needed capabilities. Will you transform current functions to support these enhanced capabilities, organically grow from scratch by finding the right leadership, acquire them through M&A-type activities, or form some kind of commercial partnership? Regardless of which sourcing strategy you choose, it's imperative you do make a choice. Some of these capabilities are in such high demand that if you wait too long, the decisions may be made for you.

When standing on the outside of a strategy office, a company's acquisitions can sometimes be misunderstood. The valuations paid for businesses, especially young companies, can appear irresponsible. But digging below the surface, you may realize that the capability gap is the motivation. Over the last several years, there have been some interesting investments from some of the world's largest companies. General Motors buying Cruise Automation has allowed it to take a significant step forward in the autonomous vehicle race. Ford investing in Pivotal gives it access to many digital service capabilities. Walmart buying Parcel allows it to begin to bridge the "last mile" delivery gap. Delta Airlines investing in Clear helps its customers have the chance to have a more seamless experience. Each of these investments is different. Some could have a much larger commercial value than others based on near-term revenue, or longer-term value based on technology portfolios. All of them, however, have the potential to shape in-demand capabilities for the connecting world.

In the end, the capability that differentiated your firm in the Unconnected World may cease being core to what your firm will be in the Connected World. If this is the case, then you may choose to eliminate the capability from inside the organization and buy it from an external market. What's important is that there are no mixed messages from leadership regarding the capabilities it's choosing as part of the company's capability future profile, and that the entire team understands why and supports it.

START PREPARING TODAY

We've talked about how leaders are sometimes reluctant to start working on capabilities because they're not ready to show a connected feature or are not entirely clear exactly how connectivity will be embraced in the future strategy. They'll claim that without data, it's impossible to build requirements, form partnerships, and find innovation in the space. It's true they don't have all of the tools at their disposal. Still, it doesn't mean you shouldn't ask your leaders what they could do today to create a structure that will mimic the moment when they're ready to show a connected feature. Don't wait. Start preparing to compete as if you're already in the Connected World. It's no different than the auto companies buying rideshare companies to test out the autonomous vehicle landscape of the future. It allows them to collect rudimentary sets of information similar to the data they'll receive from the future product. Consumers begin associating the brands with transportation instead of merely products. Now you have to encourage your team to "Live the Connected World" so they start transforming the organization's capabilities today.

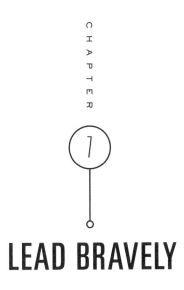

LEAD BRAVELY

"Opportunity only knocks once!"

The easy work is done. You've committed to shifting your strategies. You've identified the capabilities to match the plan, and you're willing to resource the transformation necessary. Equally important is your willingness to dampen or eliminate the legacy constraining capabilities. With the First Mile nearly complete, you're on your way to competing in the Connected World.

Still, all you have right now is a desire and plan to be a different company. Nothing externally observable has taken place. The current market for your products or services still sees your company as the one it has always been. A complete plan is necessary, but it's by no means sufficient. Implementation doesn't just happen in the executive offices. It needs to transcend the entire organization. This is the moment to reflect on the sources of organizational inertia. The organization, as of now, will continue to execute in the way it has been conditioned; employees will methodically repeat the same decisions that have historically resulted in receiving bonuses and positive feedback. Now comes the moment for executive leadership to make clear to everyone in the organization that the basis of competition is shifting and the sustainability of the organization is at risk if the company fails to respond. If the entire organization isn't on board, you can expect the old structure to constrain the transformation, and the traditional culture to ignore the elegant new plan. As seen in figure 24, now is the time to *Invest to Implement the Response.*

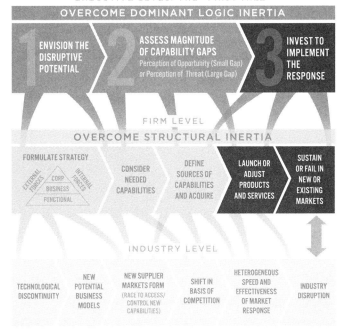

Figure 24 – CGS Connected World Transformation Framework – Invest to Implement the Response.

Inventing a company is a complex balancing process of finding the necessary resources to build internal capabilities while getting a product or service to market in order to start a revenue stream. Reinventing a company through transformation is definitely a more complex balance of shifting the capability profile of the company from a legacy set, one that has generated the legacy revenue and profit, to a new adjusted profile of capabilities. The funding source for resourcing the new capabilities usually comes from the revenue and profit generated from the legacy products and services. For companies with deep pockets or sufficient internal slack resources, the process of diverting resources is far simpler, giving them an advantage over other smaller or leaner competitors.

Companies lacking deep pockets are faced with a greater challenge when it comes to shifting resources. Some have likened the transformation to changing the tires of a car while the car is still moving. It requires retaining sufficient momentum in the marketplace with existing products and services to create in parallel the new capabilities needed to sustain the company through the mid- and long term. In some companies, owners may be asked to accept lower levels of profitability in order to reinvest in the new capabilities. Some owners may consider this an acceptable tradeoff. Others, especially those at publicly owned companies, may find it difficult to muster shareholder backing for such a move. Shareholders are not bound to their ownership and may decide to sell their interest in the company and move to invest in other companies that appear to have a brighter, more certain future. External executive boards will deem a decline in share price as unfavorable and put pressure on internal executives to right the ship. Shareholder concerns may come from external perceptions that the company is either not moving fast enough or moving too fast.

It's time for you and your fellow leaders to determine if you're willing to take on the challenge of transformation. As a CEO facing a similar transformation in an earlier era put it, "After years of being paid to coast atop a profit machine, I am now being expected to dismantle and reconfigure almost everything...except the profit." This is the leadership challenge. In the face of a clear and undeniable new future, the response options are simple and reflect the most basic human reactions: freeze, flight, or fight.

SIGNAL AND LEGITIMIZE CHANGE

The time has come for you to educate your current organization on the coming change and show everyone from the top down to the bottom why the industry you compete in is on the verge of a significant period of disruption. It's not a time for fear but for a realistic assessment of the future. Stress the unique context of the moment. One era of success is ending, and a new one is emerging. Explain why you believe the organization can emerge from the disruption—assuming you do believe it—not only as a viable company but also as an industry leader. Make clear that the greater risk is not doing anything at all. The only certainty, they must understand, is that companies failing to attempt the transformation are awaiting the outcome their competitors will ultimately assign.

The reality of the message doesn't make it an easy issue to broach, and advocating the need to transform is never an easy sell. The top levels of organizations in formerly stable industries aren't in the habit of discussing the long view. Relatively stable and predictable strategies—business and corporate—are what have allowed the company to consistently compete over the years. Sometimes companies have been managed a specific way for decades. Most of the time, they're unfamiliar with and disinterested in activities related to transformation. A decision for a legacy product company to compete based on information-based services brings all sorts of demanding questions to the forefront, such as how they will communicate the transformation to the market and what it means for the company's value. They're unaccustomed to asking such questions.

A potential barrier to signaling and legitimizing change is one of articulation. Executives who have traveled the First Mile of transformation must articulate the intellectual journey to everyone in the organization, including ownership. If they haven't completed the First Mile, then their messages will sound incomplete and no transformation will occur. If the leaders in your organization can identify the disruptive potential of the Connected World, but they can't quite articulate what new capabilities will be required and how they'll go upon acquiring them, then they'll find themselves stuck.

Leaders who haven't completed the First Mile will try to communicate the plans, but their efforts will result in goal ambiguity between the leadership and the rest of the organization. Employees will not comprehend how the new goals will impact existing ones. Most transformation efforts within organizations fail, in our opinion, because of goal ambiguity. Employees don't immediately understand how their individual goals will change as a result of the shift in corporate goals. Broad statements and new directives from executives can sow confusion instead of understanding. The solution is as simple as cascading the changes in goals throughout the entire organization to ensure all employees are up to date on how their daily activities will and won't change. They need to know some of the goals will be new, while others will be fully deleted because they're no longer relevant. Yes, needed capabilities will change, and this will be the most notable change for the workforce, yet not every specific detail of the new activities can be controlled from the top. We believe that people inherently want to succeed. They want to be part of well-thought-through change and will embrace it if they understand what winning looks like. They'll in fact run toward it.

Examples of where transformation can first be felt are often in areas of external supplier transactions. An approach could entail sitting down with the purchasing function and explaining how and why the new strategy means having to cultivate different types of relationships with suppliers. They'll need partnerships that are more collaborative than simply buying components for a physical product. If the details of the transformation aren't broken down and successfully conveyed to the workers, the function will continue to perform according to the pattern it knows.

The necessary communication isn't one-sided with a top-to-bottom approach. Cascading and feedback loops are equally important. A department head should be able to repeat back to the strategists the goals expected of the department and how they'll be met. Inside the unit, the leader will then clarify the transformation with each subunit. When there's successful iteration, the subdepartments reach out to the employees and repeat the process. This isn't merely a "feel good" exercise. It's precisely the style of communication needed across the entire organization to guarantee the alignment of the organization's new definition of success with the business strategy.

Some leaders will take to the iteration exercise well. They'll anticipate the change and throw themselves into it. They may even show initiative and come up with proposals on how they can lead differently. Other leaders will be less enthusiastic about the need for the transformation. This is a natural part of involving humans with collective efforts. A piecemeal approach where some departments realign their goals and business function output and others don't is insufficient. Delivering a business strategy, in the end, is about all the departments working in sync. The risk of not consistently communicating the change to every function in the organization is immense. Consistency of transformation at this early stage is more important than having some departments run ahead without the engagement of the other departments necessary to create a new capability. Uneven, uncoordinated change within a company creates internal friction, a metaphorical "grinding of gears," as departments redefine their internal interdependencies. This friction, a source of inertia, delays the organization's response to the marketplace. Failing to resolve the tension is a failure of executive leadership. If executives are signaling change and not everyone is absorbing it, and there are no consequences to the friction, other departments may see the efforts as a failure, which will act as further hindrance to joining the transition efforts.

As an organizational leader, you hold a lot of influence to make the changes a reality. You're not some disgruntled employee in the lunchroom who thinks he knows better than everyone how to run the company. You hold two powerful resources to paint this change in a more legitimate light: time and money. If you continue to dedicate 100 percent of your money to projects suited for the old product or service, then nobody in the organization will take your call to action seriously. On the other hand, if they see you dramatically shifting investment to achieving new capabilities, they'll quickly grasp that you're dead serious about this change. If you don't honor this new space, others won't either. They'll continue to think of connected programming as a small functional element being used to hedge a bet for the future but not something that needs attention now.

Time is the second resource at your disposal. If you and other top leadership consistently devote time in public and internal speeches to the plans for transformation, in a matter of months, it will begin to feel real to the employees. Good leaders invest the time. Average leaders expect other people to invest it. It's about being brave enough to speak and act differently today. If you can't look at the content of your speeches and recognize real shifts from how things were done last year, it means you haven't figured out a way to make the change a reality.

In the late 2000s, Google came out with their 20 percent mantra, which called on employees to devote 20 percent of their time to projects of their choosing. It was an attempt to ensure their innovative culture wasn't lost as they grew. Soon, similar programs spread across the business world. Corporate leaders called on their various groups to devote either a day per month or week to turn off the phones and meet with colleagues from other departments or hold company-wide brainstorming sessions. Sometimes this method doesn't mesh with the company's culture because the leaders at the top are still focused on today's operations. They're hoping a bottom-to-top approach will produce the innovation and strategies to save the company. It's time corporate leaders held a mirror up to themselves. If they think the coming technological discontinuity and its subsequent industry disruption are real, they should ask how much time they're spending on innovation and transformation. Even if you see yourself as a visionary but lacking in the preparation aspect of transformation, it's important you force yourself to spend time on it as a demonstration to the rest of the company.

TRANSFORMATION IS A FULL-TIME TEAM SPORT

Transforming an established company will certainly involve many different people; however, clarity around who is leading the change is critical. Transformations of any kind need clarity in purpose, approach, and most importantly, the team that is taking charge and leading the way. Too often, company leaders manage the connected activities through committees that are ill-defined and lack purpose. While there's something positive about bringing a group together to feel their way toward a common goal, the competition between various divisions can turn chaotic with costs and time quickly spiraling out of control. Leaders often start connected programs around a product or an innovation program. They soon learn they need a cross-functional team involved, so they allow for the "connected committee" to be formed. In reality, "connected," "smart," or "digital" programs are transformation programs in disguise. Transformations need teams, but they also need a brave leader to guide them down the First Mile and into the race.

THE CONNECTED COMMITTEE: THE POTENTIAL FOR TURF WARS

Many companies fall into the poor habit of having a part-time team managing their connected future. This typically begins with the leadership team agreeing to connect a product or enable a connected service. This inroad to the connected space typically will then follow one of three functional areas: engineering to guide a product, IT to guide the information, or digital marketing to guide the customer. In traditional product firms, it will begin with engineering where the budget is highest, and they have a process to evaluate and include new "features." There they'll reset the product and add all sorts of new options for the customer. Many decisions crop up as they begin working with the design team and potential partners outside the company. As it knocks through the company's pipeline all the way up to post-manufacturing, the leaders are focused on developing a product with embedded sensors, but typically nobody has given much thought about plans for the data it generates. Only when the enhanced product is near completion will they sit down and consider such questions as how the data is collected and whether it goes to the public cloud or an internal data lake. They will be a long way off from how this information will have the potential to shift other internal processes, and the real value for others beyond their current customer. At this point, you can expect a multiheaded monster to emerge, with each functional leader looking to put his or her imprint on the new product as it relates to his or her functional responsibility.

At things companies, engineering and manufacturing are used to running the show, and their interest is in meeting the requirements of the designers at the lowest possible cost. Sales is often interested in serving today's customers and making the company money now. Digital marketing approaches the product from a completely different angle. It's less concerned with the product scope and more interested in the customers' sentiments as expressed through data. It demands the flexibility to continually add new software to the product. IT wishes to ensure a suitable security layer, a platform that will scale with user growth, and the ability to properly integrate to the rest of the company's system landscape. At some point, the CIO will pipe up with opinions, arguing that many of the decisions are IT issues. Nobody at the table agrees. If the discussion isn't controlled, this ugly monster can kill the opportunity for transformation, instead stuffing a connected product into an unconnected set of processes and corporate norms.

Most teams have a coach, a place where the buck stops. It's beneficial in business to have feedback from different departments, but it's important to recognize that these various groups see the connected product through their functional lens, which has been hardened through the years. Each of these functions will likely continue to exist in the future, but they'll change. Engineering may lose influence as the likes of data emerge as the future currency of the Connected World. IT will need to shift significantly to be part of the core business and not viewed as a "back office" function. Digital marketing will need to integrate much more deeply with the customer experience and product groups. Functional leaders will not shift power and influence easily, which is why if there's no chief connected officer acting as the primary decision maker and guidepost toward a common purpose, friction will develop and slow down the transformation. Ad hoc committees aren't inherently detrimental, but they're also not sufficient to drive transformative change. Someone in the room must represent the interests of the future company and see their career more in the future than the past.

If the CEO is too ingrained in managing the current business and the responsibilities of communicating with the board, then turn to a senior leadership member to act as the chief connected officer or EVP of corporate transformation. Support this transformational leader with a management team in a separate business unit with its own P&L. Allow this person to run it like a business. The leader of this group is the person who will decide the future roles of engineering, IT, and digital marketing as the company moves from a product strategy to one based on platform services. How the company monetizes its product and services may completely change, and the functions won't know how to work in this new world. Give them the challenge to cannibalize the core business. The vision should be lofty with rules that make sense. It should be controlled and manageable. Hold meetings on a regular basis so each function knows its boundaries and responsibilities. It's about getting them comfortable in this new world and not allowing them to give in to the temptation of operating according to business as usual. If given the choice, all of these groups will ask how the connected device fits their function instead of asking the real question, which is how their function fits the connected product.

The chief connected officer can't be concerned with placating everyone's concerns before flipping the switch and initiating change. Although a common source of inertia is insufficient formulation of the change in strategy and a failure to define the new portfolio of capabilities, a second source of inertia is organizations spending too much time on planning the transformation with department leadership. Finding the balance between planning and "learn as you go" is an evergreen transformation issue. Implementation should happen sooner rather than later. It goes back to the principle of prepare, don't predict. Expect a fitful, imperfect process when trying to acquire capabilities. You may make steady progress before quickly realizing the integration with current capabilities isn't as smooth as anticipated. This is why time is of the essence, and it's crucial to adopt a philosophy closer to "learn as you go." If you want to be different in the Connected World, you'll have to change. If you're not changing, then you're not changing. Discussing change isn't the same as changing, in other words. You can't wait until every function understands and comes around to the idea of how to change.

Realize that you'll always have a "been there, done that" faction. This group of leaders looks at transformative situations and thinks they're not a big deal. After all, the organization has a finely tuned system for launching new versions of a product (product management). Most companies have experience in managing standard projects (project management). Every function and its members understand perfectly what is expected of them and each detail is planned out and executed to perfection. A well-oiled machine. There's one problem with this comparison:

This isn't a product launch.

This isn't a typical project for incremental change.

This is a complete transformation.

It may take a critical mass of people within the organization to understand where you're headed, but there's not enough time to spend endless cycles debating every aspect and convincing each person of what needs to be done. People will have to figure it out as the organization moves forward, and the only way they'll truly get the message is when they see the transformation happening full steam ahead. Some department leaders or personnel will be slow to adopt the principles of the change for a variety of reasons related to individual differences inherent among humans. The company's transformation efforts must be evaluated against the needs of individuals finding their comfort with the change. The tolerance of the executives of the company to conscientious objectors unconvinced of the need or speed of the change will vary across companies. Successful companies, however, will not allow a few unhappy employees to slow the transformation. Executives prepared for transformation will recognize that the solution lies in replacing these workers. Frequently, the replacement of the first objector to the transformation has a motivating effect on the peers of the substituted person. The peers may respond that they had not previously had the change imperative explained so clearly as when they saw it was directly related to retaining their current role.

CO-OPT ENTREPRENEURIAL DEXTERITY

In the previous chapter, we discussed the capabilities necessary to compete in the connecting world. Enterprise innovation is one capability at the core of perpetual success. This capability is the consistent application of new or unique ideas that support the enterprise's strategy and create value for the stakeholder—shareholder, customer, partner, or employee. This is the capability most needed to set the tone for future success, especially during times of industry disruption. The ultimate question, after all, is how you'll reconcile the proposed innovative transformation with the founder's intent, something that has become hardened into the current structure. As long as the company is profitable and the people who operate the company have experienced successes associated with current business models, the founder's intent is going to be hard to adjust, even when promising the innovation of a lifetime.

To drive innovation inside your firm, you may want to look outside your corporate walls. Think back to when your founder was an early entrepreneur starting the company. What you'll probably see is that like all entrepreneurs, the founder didn't sit around waiting for perfect conditions to make use of the innovation. Entrepreneurs are an impatient bunch. Often they've put all their eggs into one basket to get in the game and make adjustments as they go. Many entrepreneurs put their own financial well-being on the line. Some take second mortgages on their homes as they try and build the company. They don't have the luxury of patience, and they don't fear failure. They are brave!

When mistakes happen, entrepreneurs learn from them and move on. Most importantly, they appreciate the value of failing. Real change is about identifying innovative value and taking advantage of it. It will require "intrapreneurial" skills to navigate the corporate structure and to protect innovation from the corporate cultural antibodies. The cultural norms that exist in most established companies want to drag innovative concepts—and those who help to dream them—back into the typical value system of derisking and staying the current course. Only courageous leaders can drive toward the Connected World.

A secret weapon in the intrapreneurial fight is one directly borrowed from the entrepreneurial community. In corporations, if a product or program isn't predictable or falls too far off an originally planned course, it can be considered in "red status," or a failed initiative. In the world of the innovator, it's considered an opportunity to pivot. Pivoting involves a model of constant learning and adjusting. If you come to market with a product and quickly discover the market has no need for it but wants something similar, you need the dexterity to modify and relaunch it. Sometimes you may think you're a B2C company. After launching, the market may send signals that the better way to sell your widget is through a B2B channel. You immediately go to work and change your strategy. It's like a software company releasing the beta so it can move to version 1.0, which will allow it to finally move to version 2.0, and so on.

Pivoting isn't just difficult to execute in a massive corporation. It's usually frowned upon as an unnecessary risk to the stability of the company. People in large companies in stable industries experience whiplash from pivoting. It's night and day from the reaction to pivoting in entrepreneurial settings in immature industries where corporate agility and capturing the future are celebrated and necessary to establish some level of sustainability through dominance. This is where the principle "prepare, don't predict" proves important. You're moving to unchartered territory, and it's a moment for stark honesty. It's vital the workforce is prepared for this honesty as well. It's not the time to shut your eyes to setbacks and failures. The thought that the company may look radically different in merely one or two years is a sign the organization is moving toward the cutting edge and away from what won't work in the near future. This dynamic environment may not suit all of the employees and leaders of the legacy company. Recruiting the type of people who are comfortable working in a dynamic environment that encourages this "learn as you go" approach and "intrapreneurial" spirit is crucial.

The dictionary defines "bravery" as "the quality or state of having or showing mental or moral strength to face danger, fear, or difficulty." In battle, it may mean putting oneself in harm's way. Inside corporations, it's doing things that are frightening because the culture tells you it may limit your advancement or get you fired. Bravery is not necessarily required in a corporate culture where long-term stability and consistency in the delivery of a product or service is rewarded. The future shouldn't depend on brave executives taking risks with their careers. Pivoting requires that you and your fellow leaders recognize the need to adjust your own internal capabilities to adopt a readiness to be continuously changing and adjusting your work. It's also dependent on executives adjusting the policies and internal incentives to create a culture where the people taking risks can do so safely. Many times, people assume younger people who have less to lose must staff these types of programs, but it doesn't need to be a youth movement. It's not about a specific age but a certain mindset. Often, it's about reprogramming the norms that a multidecade career has ingrained in a leader. It may be difficult, but you can teach an old dog a new trick.

We recently attended an event for a major automotive company undergoing a major pivot. This company has decided to operate two large business units at the same time, with each one broken into smaller units. The automotive side houses the core business. Designing, producing, and distributing the product is what they do well. Meanwhile, the other business unit is planning for the Connected World. What's surprising in hearing the CEO, chairman, and leadership speak is how little they know about the makeup and activity of the second group. Yet, they were talking about pivoting, bravery, investing resources into a protective space called emerging business units, and challenging the group to come up with ways to compete in a still-unformed industry. They were comfortable with the idea it would take years to find out whether the project was a success. They've created a nurturing environment for these capabilities to materialize. They know the pivoting, fail-quickly attitude and risk taking go against how the mature organization has been operating through the years. One of the only ways to make change happen is to separate and isolate the program, drawing a distinction between your legacy business and the new portions of your company required to compete in the Connected World.

Truly transformative innovation programs rely on shareholders to relax expectations when it comes to shared value and time horizons. Owners will generally be as wrong about the future as the executives of companies for which they invest. Shareholders, however, can be quite fluid with their investments with relatively minor risks. Executives aren't as fluid with their career choices. If you as an enterprise leader are going to dip your toe in the water, you had better be serious, brave, and prepared to get wet.

CONNECT NOW

There's always going to be a compelling reason as to why now is not the right time to connect. The product isn't ready, or the current connected product can't support the transformation of the business. It's easy to tell yourself that you'll leave the idea for adaptation in the incubation and R&D state. Maybe it will be ready for the upcoming generation of leaders. Don't be the leader who thinks the steps outlined in this book sound like a great plan as soon as your product is ready. Immediately identify the portions of your business you can instruct to function like a connected company today.

The employee base is a great place to start. Create a connected employee program, and have employees begin functioning in a connected workforce. Naturally, this small internal change will infuse itself into the culture and the mindset of the functional leadership. No step is too small. If you believe autonomous is the future, then hire chauffeurs so you can start simulating some of the experiences of the future landscape. Create mobile apps that will someday be integrated into the product but for now are separate. Connect your product with aftermarket "bolt-ons." Push your departmental leadership to envision what a connected future will look like and begin outlining what the processes, information flow, and experiences will feel like. Have them explain in detail what information will come from the products, and whether some data will come from adjacent products and services. At this moment, you can simulate how the flow will look. Don't ever let the realities of design, engineering, or manufacturing cycles get in the way of your transformation.

Many companies are already doing this. Why isn't yours?

Earlier in the book, we discussed Amazon's release of the Dash button, a small device that connects via Wi-Fi to your home router and the internet. The device has a single button that when depressed performs an action. Amazon released the first generation of these buttons with a replenishing service for household goods such as laundry detergent. Jeff Bezos and his team understood there was a promise of "connected appliances" that will self-replenish, even if this future of connected features in appliances were still several years away from being manufactured in scale. Instead of waiting, Amazon simulated the connected experience using inexpensive technology that could be adhered to an appliance already in the home. The Dash button doesn't fully adhere to the promise of the frictionless experience of a self-ordering appliance, but it does prepare Amazon for that day. It strikes partnerships with goods manufacturers, hones the supply chain, produces consumption data for Amazon customers, and begins to train the customer base to expect on-demand deliveries.

Similarly, automotive dealerships will have massive changes when the autonomous vehicle becomes a reality. Cars could drive to dealerships, check themselves in, be serviced, and drive home. How many automotive dealers are ready for this new era? Dealers can begin readying today by incentivizing customers to check themselves in remotely or make remote payments without human interaction. They'll learn how to tune the experience and be ready for when the autonomous vehicle eventually arrives.

What parts of your company's value chain will the Connected World likely disrupt? What prevents you from disrupting them today to begin the transformation?

BEGIN COLLABORATING NOW TO GAIN PERSPECTIVE

For the top leadership, these steps mean not taking an insular approach to the journey. Speak with other market leaders who are experiencing the same challenges. The scope of the coming change is greater than any single firm and goes beyond any industry. Use the tools of leadership at your disposal to get involved with others who are trying to answer these same questions. C-level executives should use the outward-facing responsibilities and benefits of the job to observe, learn, and partner with the entities that will provide them with solutions they can take back home. Many senior executives inside companies already sit on advisory and governing boards of companies and educational institutions. Seek out organizations different from yours. If you're a things company, then look to get involved with the board of a digital company. Consider taking a role at a university where interesting research is happening in related fields.

The executives at Apple, for instance, sit on boards of organizations not at all connected to Silicon Valley digital companies. This provides them with an opportunity to hear of issues, challenges, or solutions that maybe haven't yet reached their company or industry. It's not an approach only for executives at large public companies. If you're at a private company, you can take an advisory position at a different private organization. You can also arrange meet-ups with other small business leaders inside and outside your space.

If you're a functional leader, now may be the moment to delegate many of your current operational responsibilities to your lieutenant so you are freer to spend time gaining exposure to ideas outside the company and industry. If you're not comfortable in that role, then ask the second in charge to be the person going out and meeting people and companies. The point is to sit with people who are seeing many of these same challenges through a different lens and from a different angle.

Another option is to assemble a group of enterprise innovators, the people who lead the innovation teams at their firms. Some companies think they've found a great way to innovate within their industries, sourcing the technologies that will allow them to compete. Still, they know that most of the change for the Connected World will happen beyond the digitization their own products are currently undergoing. They understand that innovation for their firms will happen on the fringes of their current industries. The realization forces them to cross traditional industry lines and seek collaborative innovation.

This is what we're doing in Detroit with a group called Connected Detroit Innovates. It's not just about bringing like-minded innovators together. Rather, it's also about learning how to collaborate. It's a preinvestment in connected collaboration, where we reverse the model. We're not waiting for the innovations to appear and then seeing whether the market allows for an opportunity to collaborate. Instead, we're encouraging companies to first get comfortable with collaboration. Next, they can see whether there are specific opportunities to work together to enter the market.

This regional project proves the power of using groups to supplement each leader's individual thinking. Group ideation creates trust between the different organizations. Once the ideas and trust form, leaders can find another company in the group that's a good match in terms of challenges and strategies. They can then break off into a smaller group to begin considering how the innovations fit into their own strategies. This smaller group can even plan proofs of concepts to run together. The collaboration is happening before looking into the problems and solutions.

Health care, for example, is moving outside hospitals. Providers are trying to figure out how to deliver care more effectively and efficiently into people's homes. Meanwhile, retailers are looking at the e-commerce market, wondering how they'll survive in the near future. These health-care and retail companies are essentially facing the same issues. Sitting in the same room, they can think about experiments to implement, or how to use certain innovations. They may use an idea from one of the companies and come up with a partnering agreement or choose to start a new company together. Sometimes an idea grows and dies in a single session, which should also be celebrated as a success. Speed, after all, is the critical success factor in an age where data and information is the new currency of business success. Are you ready to sprint?

CONCLUSION

"Live your life with no regrets!"

You've done it. You've reached the end, although like most ends, this is really just another beginning. It's the beginning of a transformative journey for your industry, your firm, and for you as the leader. What you've finished reading is a reflective framework (represented in figure 25) and multistep guide that is intended to help you lead your organization through the technological discontinuity and the industry disruption it brings.

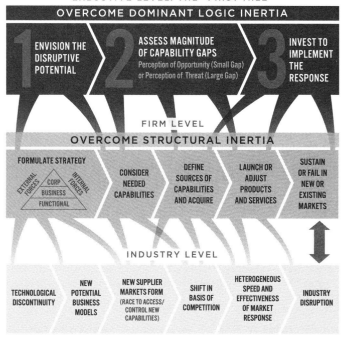

Figure 25 – CGS Advisors Core Transformation Framework.

The pages of this book are full of explanations and examples, but in the end, the process is a simple formula:

1. Envision the Disruptive Potential
    A. Understand the technological discontinuity.
    B. Understand the new potential business models.
    C. Assess the impact on your industry.
    D. Formulate your strategy and ensure you access the needed capabilities.
2. Assess the Magnitude of Capability Gaps
    A. Determine capability gaps.

B. Consider the opportunities and threats for your firm based on your perceived gaps.

C. Understand the new supplier markets and competitive race to control in-demand capabilities.

D. Understand the new basis of competition.

E. Determine your available resources to commit to fill the gap.

3. Invest to Implement the Response

A. Understand the heterogeneous nature of the market response.

B. Overcome the inertia that may slow you down.

C. Be brave and lead through the transformation.

The time has come to open your eyes and look out into the world. Determine the ideal place for your organization in the emerging landscape. How will the corporate, business, and functional strategies you develop help your organization assume that role? Don't simply identify the capabilities needed to assume the role. Build a transformational management team to implement the required changes. Accept and embrace the possibility of having to look outside the company for those capabilities. Most importantly, be the engine of change, not the trailer weighing down progress.

Make the transformation visible and known, not a secret known to only you. Consider creating a poster-sized image of the transformation framework and hanging it outside your office. We do this in almost all of the transformations we support to allow for visual recognition of where you, your team, and your company are headed. Bring it to the next board meeting, show it to the other executives, or present it at the next Rotary Club gathering. This is a way to open yourself to reactions from leaders in a no-risk environment. If you're not motivated to get the conversation started, then you'll never be prepared to compete in the Connected World. The Connected World will transform all people through all of their lives. It will transform society, and not getting started on your preparation is just a way of deciding not to participate in the change. You can't avoid it, but you don't want to end up reacting to it and not being the leader shaping it. It's our hope that after reading this book—or even in the middle of reading it—you'll not only feel motivated to launch your organization on this journey, but you'll also have the insight to find the right path to fit your needs. The book will be a success for us if you decide to act one day, month, quarter, or year earlier than you would have if you hadn't read the book.

The clients we advise are at various stages of this journey. Some of them we meet at the beginning as they struggle to make sense of their changing industry, while others come to us near the end as they face great internal resistance to their attempt at enhancing capabilities. Every firm, after all, comes with an existing culture, founder's intent, history, and profile capability. Surely, they'll find certain parts of the journey easier than others. They may have built-in proficiencies to get through certain stages with little effort. But what happens when they encounter resistance? Facing complications is what can lead to delay, which is, as we've discussed, the ultimate factor in determining your position in the Connected World. You and your organization can't afford to get stuck for long on any one stop of this journey. Recognize your paralysis and engage someone who can help you move forward.

Outside assistance can come in many different forms. You may be a natural change leader, in which case, all you'll require is a coach figure to provide occasional encouragement and guidance. Certain MBA programs provide courses on transformation and some of the issues discussed in this book. In fact, we lecture in some of them, and auditing these classes may be enough to pull you and your organization through to the other side. Nevertheless, it's important to recognize when you'll need a trusted group to come in and structure the transformation and even manage a portion of it themselves. If your entire career has been about operations, then there's no embarrassment in admitting change will necessitate an experienced partner.

This book doesn't come from a place of malice toward the willfully blind executives we wrote about in chapter 3, "Change or Die." We don't think leaders are incompetent and unaware. We believe you and your fellow leaders are good and want to do right by your company. We've always led with the belief that people inherently wish to succeed. They want to support change but need to be given the clarity to understand what is being asked of them. Being hopeful for the opportunities, yet frightened by the journey toward the Connected World and its implications is understandable. In our years of working in this area of transformation, it's become clear to us that leaders want to succeed. They just often don't know how. It's not even that they're afraid of change. They're afraid of not knowing how the change will make them successful. They'll begin the journey once they believe it will lead to goodness. Nobody, after all, wants to be part of a sinking ship.

We are, however, realists. We know it's not going to be all smooth sailing. You'll encounter bumps in the road. Although we're encouraging you to move swiftly, we suggest you step back from time to time and observe the macro-patterns. A friendly client calls these sessions "forest meetings." It's forced time for you and your leadership to see the forest distinctly from the trees. Changing course and swapping out capabilities will eventually affect people. People are worth the time. Be aware that some of these technological changes will deemphasize the need for massive sets of generic functions. Just as automation in factories has reshaped hands-on manufacturing, automation in cars and trucks will reshape careers tied to driving. Automation in retail will reshape many jobs from the warehouse to the checkout lane. You'll need to understand how these shifts will affect your employees and, even more importantly, large classes of people who are disproportionately tied to these type of jobs. The largest percentage of jobs for African Americans in the United States, for example, is connected to driving (cars, trucks, tractors, forklifts, etc.). As leaders, we have a responsibility to our company, our employees, and to our communities. One of our great friends, Tim McCabe, reminds people that great leadership comes with great responsibility. As a former officer at a Global 100 company, he explains how corporate decisions can affect multiple generations of citizens. You'll need to be swift and thoughtful as you navigate this connected journey.

We do believe it's going to be a better world, and we hope you can develop the same optimism. It's not going to be filled with only entrepreneurs and new entrants. The traditional companies that employ thousands of people and are the bedrocks of the country and the communities where they are located can have a place in the changing world. It's our hope that we can help you and every other leader pivot as effortlessly as possible.

As you embark on your journey, we invite you to share your problems and progress with us so we can provide you with encouragement, assistance, and viable solutions. Guiding companies through this journey is what we do. When we're not preparing the next generation of business leaders for the challenges of technical disruption, we are speaking to current leaders at conferences and meeting with them one-on-one to try and tackle some of their most vexing problems. The Connected World will cause disruption, but it doesn't mean we need to react with fear. This should be a moment of excitement, where a rising tide lifts all boats, and where we lean on each other for support during this transformative and exciting journey. Good luck. Be brave. Live life with no regrets!

WHO WE ARE

GREGGORY R. GARRETT is the founder and CEO of CGS Advisors, LLC, a boutique strategic transformation and innovation advisory firm serving clients globally. He has always pushed the limits of cultures by formulating and implementing unique market-disrupting strategies. An accomplished leader, Gregg takes pride in recognizing commonsense solutions for complex and systemic problems and supports "corporate bravery" by motivating teams to reach well beyond the typical boundaries in order to achieve greatness.

Recognizing the complexity of emerging macroeconomic ecosystems, Gregg has recently led the launch of Connected Detroit Innovates, a cross-industry consortium of chief innovation officers who are committed to collaborating in an effort to succeed in the Connected World.

Gregg's academic training, rooted in systems engineering, was enhanced with an MBA focused on integrative management. He spent close to a decade as a consultant at Ernst & Young before moving to leadership positions at Volkswagen and Deutsche Telekom. In his last role before founding CGS Advisors, Gregg was the chief strategy officer for IT and innovation at Volkswagen in North America, where he developed and led the digital strategy and innovation practice for one of the largest automotive companies in the world.

Throughout his twenty-five-plus years in product, telecom, IT, and advisory services industries, Gregg has been occupied with the questions and challenges surrounding change and transformation. In the beginning of his career, he was identified as a problem solver. After years of studying crises and predicaments, he developed an eye for identifying systemic opportunities before they emerged.

Gregg is a maker. He founded his first firm at the age of sixteen, a collegiate lacrosse program by twenty, and his first industry consortium by twenty-nine. Gregg is also a teacher. He has coauthored a Harvard Business School case, keynoted and spoken at more than fifty global conferences, and is an adjunct faculty and lecturer at several business and engineering schools. As a leader, Gregg sits on several corporate advisor boards, chaired a not-for-profit association, and has been coaching since he was fourteen years old.

Gregg's unique blend of professional management experiences in corporate settings, entrepreneurism, systemic understanding of enterprises, and knowledge of upcoming technologies makes him passionate about two distinct areas:

- The Connected World: The evolving ultraconnected environment of people AND products will revolutionize the world economy over the next ten years.
- People: The best strategies are useless unless people are motivated to understand and implement them.

Gregg is a dedicated father to two sons and the husband to his wife, Amy, who continuously encourages him to live life with no regrets.

DR. WARREN RITCHIE, after more than thirty-five years of work is moving progressively and deliberately into retirement, stepping away from the internal bustle of organizations. He intends to continue with advisory projects where the involved people are passionate and the issues interesting.

Warren has worked in the public sector, academia, and the private sector in civil aviation, technology, and automotive industries. He has accumulated bachelor's, master's, and doctoral degrees from universities in Canada and the United States. Warren has taken roles across multiple functional areas including sales, marketing, finance, supply chain, strategy, and IT. During his years in corporations, he rose to C-level executive roles in multiple functional areas.

Post the corporate world, Warren became an independent business consultant who contributed to the start-up of CGS Advisors and for a time was the CGS practice leader for strategy services. He remains a contributor to the CGS Fellows Program.

His next goal is to perfect the double haul cast and explore some of the saltwater flats of the world.

The two authors began collaborating in 2002 when Gregg joined a Volkswagen Group consulting services company and partnered with Warren who was responsible for a massive corporate strategy initiative that included the transformation of the IT function. They quickly discovered that their unique viewpoints on how companies transform in disrupted industries played off each other to exceptional results. The partnership blossomed as they carried their transformation program globally through North and South

America and eventually Europe. Although finding separate paths for a few years, Warren and Gregg continued to support each other with considering different approaches to complex issues. In 2008, the partnership deepened when Warren, who was then the CIO at Volkswagen, brought over Gregg to become the chief strategy office for IT and innovation. Four years later, Warren joined Gregg who had launched Corporate Growth Strategy (CGS) Advisors, a boutique strategic transformation and innovation advisory firm whose chief focus is helping clients globally prepare for industry disruption caused by emerging technologies. CGS Advisors supports companies as they identify unique paths to growth and facilitate internal transformations so they can stay competitive in the Connected World.

This book aims to share Gregg and Warren's experiences, knowledge, and approach with a broad group of leaders who may not have direct access to the classrooms where they teach, or their boutique advisory firm.